MEMORY AND AWARENESS

A Series of Books in Psychology

Editors:
Richard C. Atkinson
Gardner Lindzey
Richard F. Thompson

MEMORY AND AWARENESS

An Information-Processing Perspective

Roberta L. Klatzky

W. H. Freeman and Company
New York

Credits

Figure 2.2   Figure 3, in J. L. McClelland and D. E. Rumelhart. "An interactive activation model of context effects in letter perception. Part 1. An account of basic findings." *Psychological Review,* 1981, vol. 88, pp. 375–407. Copyright 1981 by the American Psychological Association. Reprinted by permission of the author.

Figure 3.1   Data from Table 3 in: C. McCauley, et al. "Early extraction of meaning from pictures and its relation to conscious identification." *Journal of Experimental Psychology: Human Perception and Performance,* 1980, vol. 6, pp. 265–276. Copyright 1980 by the American Psychological Association. Adapted by permission of the author.

Figure 3.3   Figure 2 from: Crossman, E. R. F. W. "A theory of the acquisition of speed-skill." *Ergonomics*, 1959, vol. 2, pp. 153–166.

Figure 6.2   Figure 3 from: E. K. Warrington & H. J. Sanders. The fate of old memories. *Quarterly Journal of Experimental Psychology,* 1971, vol. 23, pp. 432–442. (Academic Press, Inc., London).

Library of Congress Cataloging in Publication Data

Klatzky, Roberta L.
  Memory and awareness.

  (A Series of books in psychology)
  Bibliography: p.
  Includes index.
  1. Memory.   2. Awareness.   3. Human information
processing.   I. Title.   II. Series.
  BF371.K533   1984   153.1′2   84-4017

ISBN 0-7167-1599-6
ISBN 0-7167-1600-3 (pbk.)

Printed in the United States of America

1 2 3 4 5 6 7 8 9 0

To Jim Geiwitz

Preface

This book originated from several sources. Foremost among them was a body of new research that seemed to converge on awareness as a central construct. This research included studies of developmental changes in children's knowledge about memory, attempts to demonstrate perceptual processing without awareness, clinical reports about amnesic patients, experiments on adults' understanding of the sources of their recollections and indeed, their understanding of memory in general, and a burgeoning literature on motor performance. Through my own research, I became increasingly interested in people's extraordinary inability to articulate virtually anything of how they remembered faces—a phenomenon related to awareness as well as face recognition. New applications for the theories and empirical findings of cognitive psychology were another impetus. Many of these applied topics also touched on awareness, often with direct acknowledgment, but equally often without it. The applied issues that seemed relevant included computer simulations of experts' performance, psychologists in the courtroom, the development and maintenance of skill, and tacit influence of advertisements. In conducting a seminar with graduate students at the University of California at Santa Barbara, I became increasingly cognizant of the relationships among these diverse topics. This book is my attempt to describe both the topics and relationships, and in so doing, to provide at least the outlines of memory and awareness as a substantive focus within the information-processing approach to psychology.

The organization of the book is as follows: Chapter 1 presents an overview of memory and awareness, as well as some preliminary theoretical and methodological considerations. A description of human memory from the information-processing perspective is given in Chapter 2. Chapters 3–6 expand on a typology of awareness presented in Chapter 1. Each chapter deals with a set of related phenomena, describing relevant research and theory, and touching on applications. Chapter 7 is the requisite summing up. This book assumes no extensive background in either experimental psychology or theories of memory. Experimental techniques are generally described in as much detail as necessary to grasp their implications, and relevant background information about memory is provided by Chapter 2. By these means I hope to make recent advances in the psychology of awareness available to a wide audience.

I gratefully acknowledge the support of the Center for Advanced Study in the Behavioral Sciences, where *Memory and Awareness* was largely written. That support includes my co-Fellows, who had to listen to many of my ideas still in their raw stages. In particular, the "memory mavens"—Gus Craik, Bob Crowder, Matt Erdelyi, Salvador Luria, Nancy Stein and Tom Trabasso—were a patient and constructive audience. Erdelyi and Craik also reviewed the manuscript and offered many helpful comments. I also thank my other reviewers, Marcia Johnson and George Mandler. Margaret Amara and Bruce Harley of the Center library were simply indispensable, and I greatly appreciate their help. My editor, W. Hayward Rogers, was, as always, strongly encouraging. I thank Jim Geiwitz for his friendship and intellectual camaraderie. Finally, I acknowledge financial support from National Science Foundation Grant No. BNS8206304 and the Spencer Foundation during my tenure at the Center for Advanced Study.

Roberta L. Klatzky
September 1, 1983

Contents

1

An Introduction to Memory and Awareness

AWARE: Marked by realization, perception, or knowledge: *conscious, sensible, cognizant.* Aware may indicate either general information, wide knowledge, interpretive power, or vigilant perception. Cognizant may imply the gradual impingement of knowledge or perception on one's consciousness or may connote special efforts to know. Conscious may indicate impingement on one's mind so that one recognizes the fact or existence of something. It may also indicate an extreme and dominating realization. . . . Sensible may apply to situations in which a thing is intuitively sensed and also to those in which it is rationally perceived, known, and admitted.
AWARENESS: the quality or state of being aware.

> (Webster's Third New International Dictionary (unabridged). Springfield, Mass., G. & C. Merriam Co., 1965.)

In 1911 the French psychologist Claparède described a "curious experiment" he had performed on a patient suffering from Korsakoff's syndrome, a memory disorder associated with acute alcoholism. This patient could remember very little of her life since the onset of her illness; she could not remember where she had spent every day of the last five years or the name of the doctor she saw daily. On one occasion Claparède concealed a pin in his fingers, reached for the patient's hand, and stuck her with it. Later, when reaching out again, he observed that the patient withdrew her hand. Pressed for an explanation, she could say only, "Sometimes pins are hidden in people's hands."

A speaker of Russian is learning to read English, a language with an entirely different alphabet from his native Cyrillic. Reading *the*, he slowly moves his lips from *tuh* to *heh* to *ee* positions, pausing between each, and only later recognizing the word as irregular in pronunciation. A native speaker of English is asked to circle every instance of the letter *t* in a passage of text. He misses several instances of the *t* in *the*, but not in *thy*.

A group of college students is instructed to learn words in a list by two methods: For certain words, the instructions are to repeat the item over and over again; for others, the instructions are to study by forming a mental image of the word's meaning. When asked to predict how well they will recall the words, the students state that the words will be remembered equally well, whether they were repeated or imagined. But the imagined words are remembered much better.

These three anecdotes illustrate three different aspects of the relation between memory and awareness. Claparède's patient "remembers" being stuck with a pin, in some sense; at least she knows that some people have been stuck with pins. But she appears to be unaware that this knowledge is a personal memory. The students who cannot predict that they will remember more imagined words than rotely repeated words are unaware of a general rule of memory behavior, even though evidence of it is implicit in their own performance. The native speakers of Russian and English present still another aspect of memory awareness. To the Russian, reading *the* is a laborious, intensely conscious process; he could articulate quite well (albeit in Russian) how he has come to read *the*, and he would be disrupted in his reading if he were given another task. To the native English speaker, reading *the* is an effortless process that is so far removed from a letter-by-letter articulation that the *t* merges with the *h* and *e* to form a unit.

Humans acquire new information, and subsequently use it to remember or perform, by immensely complex means. Some of these complex processes are consciously experienced; some are not. Some are understood to follow a lawful order; some seem mysterious and incomprehensible. Sometimes individuals know what they can remember; sometimes they do not. This book describes various aspects of understanding and experiencing memory from the perspective of psychological theories of the human memory system.

The present discussion of awareness and memory uses the terminology and theories of the information-processing approach to memory. A basic tenet of information-processing theories is that the human memory system can be seen as a set of structures representing information and a set of processes acting on that information. Processes can be complex and composed of subprocesses that act together under a set of rules that impose order and control. As information is processed, its form or content may change, so that it is given a different representation at different states or "stages" of processing.

In the past, information-processing theories of memory have incorporated awareness primarily as an incidental component. More recently, however, the outlines of "memory and awareness" as a research topic in its own right have become increasingly delineated by a growing body of experimentation, clinical observation, and theory. This book aims to make these outlines less shadowy, by describing topics within this emerging area and tracing potential connections among them. The discussion will stay within the information-processing framework, largely bypassing the older literature on consciousness and introspection. Were it not to do so, the task would become unmanageable.

TYPES OF AWARENESS

This book will broadly examine the three general types of awareness of memory reflected in the anecdotes that opened this chapter. One is the experiencing of the here and now that is often called "consciousness." The term "consciousness" carries with it many senses and connotations, mystical and psychoanalytical as well as those related to information processing. Its use in this text will be restricted to mean awareness of the ongoing processing of information Although it is restricted, this sense of the word is by no means narrow. It includes awareness of reactions to sensory stimulation, of motor control and execution, and of the mental activities involved in perceiving, remembering, reasoning, and other cognitive performances. To make the present sense of the term more explicit, I will borrow from a more contemporary phrase and refer to this experiencing of the here-and-now as "on-line" awareness. ("On-line awareness," however, is syntactically—not to mention aesthetically—intractable, and I will also use the terms "consciousness" and "conscious experience".)

Williams James (1890) made a distinction between conscious awareness of events occurring in the *present* and a reevocation of *past* experiences that had dropped out of consciousness and were "revived anew" in the act of remembering. Cognizance of past experiences that are stored in memory constitutes the second type of awareness of memory considered here. Sometimes we are aware of the contents of memory because we can revive, or "retrieve," them and call them into conscious experience.

At other times, a complete reawakening may be impossible, but we can still have feelings about what we know, based on whatever relevant information can be retrieved. I may feel that I would recognize the name of a high school classmate, even though I cannot recall it right now, because I can imagine her face and remember that she, too, was a member of the band. We may know not only what we know, but where we learned it, and whether it derives from reality or imagination. I refer to awareness of the contents of memory, in all of these forms, as "epistemic awareness" (after epistemology, the theory of knowledge).

Another way in which we are "aware" of memory is as a general human capacity. We all hold certain beliefs about the nature and workings of human memory and about our own peculiar memory-related abilities relative to those of others. This set of beliefs, our third type of awareness, will be called a "personal memory model." Presumably, we derive these assumptions from our own experiences and from the publicized experiences of others. We may also study memory more formally by reading a text or a popular self-help book. To the extent that individuals derive their personal memory models from common sources, and by similar processes of inference, their personal models will have certain beliefs in common. Those beliefs form a "folk knowledge" about memory. Folk knowledge may at times be invalid, but even then it is a form of awareness, in the sense that people know they have certain beliefs and can articulate them.

The three types of awareness distinguished here can be seen to differ in their proximity to immediate experience. The first, on-line awareness, concerns ongoing perceptual, cognitive, and motoric activities. The second, epistemic awareness, is an end product of information-processing activities that may or may not be consciously experienced. It will be described as the result of memory search processes (which access stored knowledge) and decision processes (which use what is accessed to produce some reportable awareness of what is known). Personal memory models, constituting the third type of awareness, are abstractions based on many prior memory-related experiences. They may derive from complex inference processes and may comprise generalizations about other people's memories as well as one's own. There is a rough correspondence between these three types of awareness and what the dictionary calls consciousness, cognizance, and sensibility. Consciousness, as Webster's would have it, "impinges;" cognizance is a more gradual enlightment based on special efforts to know; and sensibility about memory includes what is "rationally" known and admitted.

PRELIMINARY CONCERNS

Information-processing approaches to memory are relatively new, and theorists who take this approach generally rely on data from well-controlled experimental studies. Yet, any psychologist who wants to discuss awareness confronts the awesome presence of centuries of discussion, in which experimental techniques have often been given a subsidiary role. It is decisively not the purpose here to renew or review these controversies. (The early history of the study of consciousness and the status of introspective techniques can be found in Boring's (1950) classic *A History of Experimental Psychology*. More recent reviews are in Danziger, 1980; Lieberman, 1979; and Mandler, 1975.) Yet two fundamental questions related to awareness and memory cannot be ignored: What mental structures or activities correspond to awareness, and what is the appropriate method for determining what one is aware of?

With respect to the first question, information-processing theories have been concerned with the site of awareness in the "on-line" or consciousness sense, and they appear to have provided three candidates: consciousness can be viewed as 1) a sort of homunculus or "executive" controlling the flow of information through various processing stages, 2) as a particular stage of processing, or 3) as a state that representations of information can enter.

The idea that consciousness is an executive controller seems particularly problematic. For one thing, it is not clear what information-processing activities should be considered as executive functions. In many models depicting the flow of processing in some task, the homunculus incorporates those components that are not well understood. This has led Newell (1980) to suggest that information-processing theories should take as a goal " banishment of the homunculus," by which he means reducing the role that the concept of an executive controller plays. Fuller understanding of "executive functions" should lead to their being more centrally incorporated into information-processing models as principled and predictable components. Ultimately, the managing of a well understood processing task should be likened to the control of blood flow in the heart, which proceeds in an orderly fashion by constraints inherent in the apparatus itself, not through the action of some external valvekeeper.

More important, even control processes that are appropriately assigned to the executive may not come into awareness. A later chapter will discuss more fully the distinction between procedural knowledge, which may be directly implemented without awareness, and declarative knowledge, which is capable of articulation. Executive functions might be like procedural knowledge.

This leaves two remaining candidates for the site of consciousness in information-processing—the idea that it is either a stage or a state. (The stage view usually associates consciousness with "short-term memory," and the state view, with "focal attention," terms that will be explained in Chapter 2.) Although these two ideas are very closely related, and it is somewhat misleading to make a strong distinction between them, I agree with many theorists and favor the "state" depiction of consciousness (see Carr, 1979; Mandler, 1975; Posner & Klein, 1973; Underwood, 1979). The idea of a state of consciousness is especially attractive because it implies flexibility. Representations and processes might become conscious to varying degrees, according to what extent they enter this state. As we shall see, experiments suggest that we should attribute this flexibility to consciousness in information-processing.

Where to put consciousness in theoretical depictions of the human memory system should not, however, be given too much emphasis. As White (1980) has pointed out, there is a tendency to feel that assigning a location to consciousness somehow explains it. The present concern is more with its role in memory function than with its location.

The second critical question about the study of awareness—how to measure it—is more difficult to answer. As we shall see, in one form or another, verbalization is the principal measure of awareness, yet the status of verbal reports is a controversial one and their use requires some justification. We should note first that verbal report, or some motoric response that bears a direct relationship to words (such as pressing a button designated "yes"), is the principal response in information-processing psychology, whether or not awareness is the topic under study. Verbal reports, in this sense, include recalled words or labels, reports that two items are the same or different, reports that an event did or did not occur, reports that a current event is the same as a previous one in some sense, and verbalization of names for perceived events. These are all conventional and widely accepted behaviors to measure in experimental psychology, and the use of them generally causes little argument. They are verbal reports about the *outcomes* of information-processing activities, as produced in the course of some experimental task.

In addressing awareness, however, there is another, more questionable kind of verbal report to consider. This is verbalization about introspections, that is, about the nature of the information-processing activities themselves. Suppose I want to know about the information structures and processes used in mental arithmetic, for example, and I ask people

SOURCE ACTIVITIES

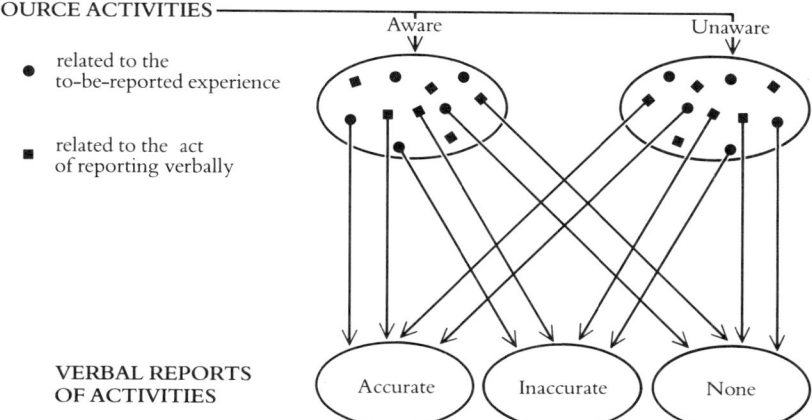

● related to the
   to-be-reported experience

■ related to the act
   of reporting verbally

VERBAL REPORTS
OF ACTIVITIES

Figure 1.1   A situation in which verbal reports cannot be used as indicators of information-processing activities.

to add 2543 and 6781 and tell me what they were aware of while doing the task. Verbal reports of this sort have had a rather uneven status in the history of psychology (Boring, 1950; Lieberman, 1979). At one time they were a basic research method; at another, they were overshadowed by the dictum that psychologists must measure behaviors, not introspections (even though many of the behaviors were verbal); and more recently, they are again advocated as a reasonable psychological research tool, when used in conjunction with others.

Why are introspective reports so controversial? Two general problems with using verbal reports as indicators of awareness, as summarized by Mandler (1975), are that the internal activities used for verbalization may themselves change the experiences one is aware of, and that verbal reports of an experience may not adequately account for what was actually experienced.

These problems may potentially result in the unfortunate situation depicted in Figure 1.1, which describes the information-processing activities used in a task of interest to a researcher, and about which participants are to make introspective reports. The figure illustrates two categories of information-processing activities: those related to the task of primary interest, that is, the task that the participants are supposed to be describing (like mental arithmetic), and activities related to the task of verbalizing. Within each of these categories, there are mental activities participants are aware of, and other of which they are unaware. The participants' behavior can be divided into three categories: accurate verbal reporting, inaccurate reporting, or no verbalization.

In the worst possible scenario of Figure 1.1, one simply cannot use verbal reports to indicate internal information-processing activities, because any type of activity can correspond to any (or no) type of report. People may fail to report their mental activities even though they are aware of them, perhaps because they are hard to verbalize, perhaps through laziness. Someone may have the impression of visualizing the carrying operation in mental addition, for example, but not find the words to describe the visual image. People may produce inaccurate reports for the same reasons. When they are unaware of internal activities, participants may produce verbal reports based on guessing, inference-making, or simple confabulation about what is going on in the mind. These reports may be accurate by chance, but often they are not. And finally, participants' reports may jumble together activities related to the task of primary interest and those related to making a verbal report. They may report thinking of the sounds of the numbers during addition, but actually do so only because they have been asked to report the numbers aloud.

The situation, however, may not be as indeterminate as Figure 1.1 makes it appear. There are several reasons to be more optimistic about verbal reports of the introspective variety. For one, such reports are generally examined in conjunction with other tasks producing alternative measures of processing, verbal or nonverbal, which provide evidence about the validity of the reports. Also, even inaccurate introspections may be of interest; for example, in studying folk knowledge about memory, which can be valid or invalid. Finally, theories of the human information-processing system suggest constraints on the use of verbal reports that increase the likelihood of their being accurate reflections of conscious information-processing activities.

Ericsson and Simon (1980) directly addressed these constraints on the accuracy of verbalization about information processing in an influential paper that advocated using "verbal reports as data." Their basic assumption is that verbalization corresponds to an externalization, or bringing out, of information currently under a particular state in the human memory system. That state will be called here "focal attention," and it will be assumed to be directly related to conscious experience. Thus, we can translate the Ericsson/Simon assumption as saying that verbal report externalizes information that is in the conscious state. Yet another formulation, accepted by Ericsson and Simon, is that the verbalized information is in a site within the memory system called "short-term memory." (As noted above, focal attention and short-term memory are very similar constructs.)

To return to the Ericsson/Simon model, the nature of what is verbalized depends on the nature of what is in the critical state (in short-term memory or under focal attention) and, equally important, how it got there. One possibility is that the information in the attentional state is in what is called a "phonemic" form; that is, it is like an implicit way of speaking and need only be articulated to come out verbally. Another possibility is that the information under attention is in a nonphonemic form that requires some translation prior to its being articulated. For example, it might be a visual image.

Whether the verbalized information under attention is in an implicit-speech form or some other form depends in part on the information-processing task that led to its being there in the first place. Some tasks may produce phonemic information directly, as an essential part of their performance. The best example is the task of reading a printed word. Other tasks, however, do not produce verbalizeable information—at least of the sort desired by an experimenter—in any direct way. In these cases, when verbalization is requested, the participant must expend some information-processing effort on the act of verbalization per se. The nature of this effort varies, depending on how available the verbalized material is.

These considerations lead Ericsson and Simon to distinguish among three "levels" of verbal report concerning information-processing tasks. These levels vary in how directly (and accurately) the verbalization reflects the information-processing activities being reported. (See Figure 1.2.) Level 1 is the most direct relationship: in this situation, the processing task of primary interest produces a directly verbalizeable output, which is directly reported. In Level 2, the primary task produces some attended-to information that is not itself phonemic but can be translated into words in a direct manner. In Level 3, the primary task does not produce the required verbal material in any direct way, but instead, the participant must make use of intermediate processes to produce the report. Further distinctions can be made according to the nature of the intermediate processes, which can include filtering out information that is under attention but is not to be verbalized (for example, when reporting only certain objects in a scene); searching for information that is not normally attended to and bringing it under attentional focus; and making complex inferences about the probable nature of information-processing activities.

An important point is that the greater the amount of intermediate processing that intervenes between some primary task and report about

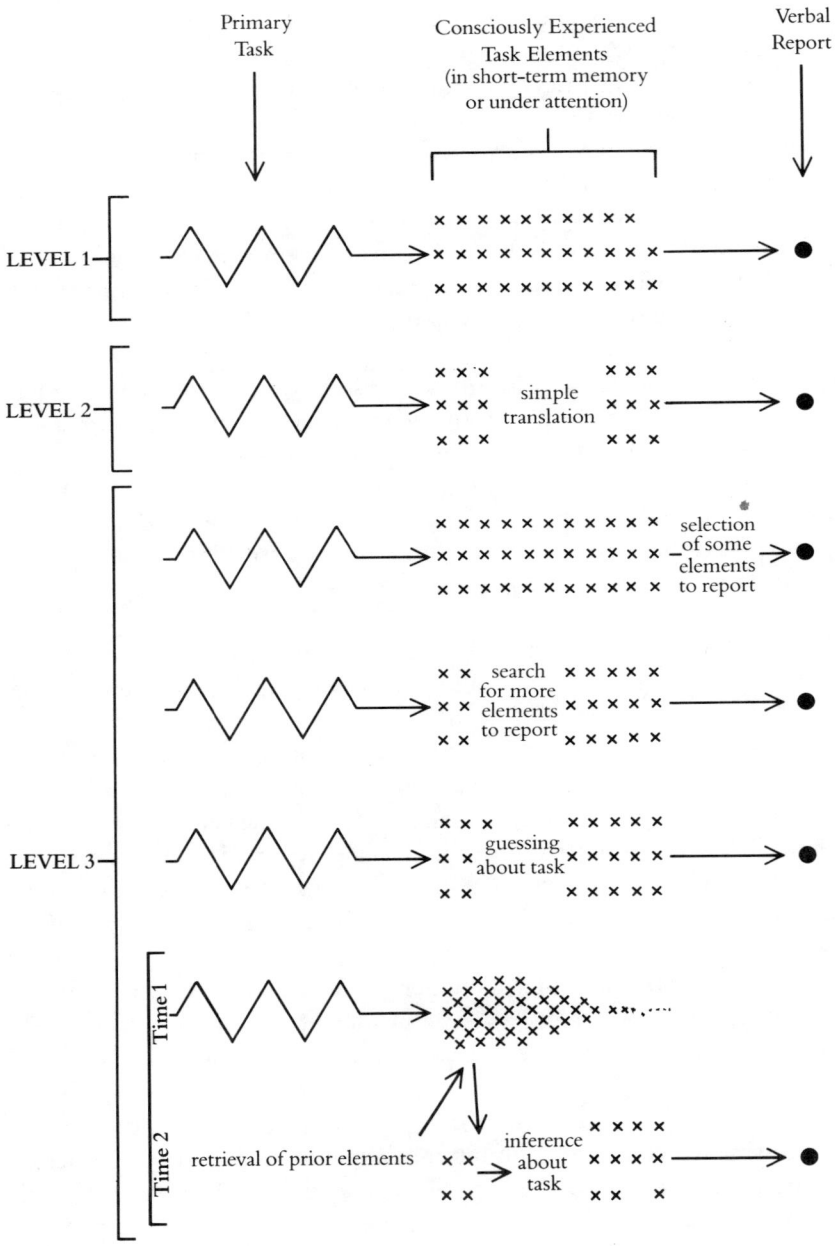

Figure 1.2   Levels of verbal report, as described by Ericsson and Simon (1980), about some primary information-processing task.

that task, the greater the likelihood that the report will be inaccurate. This becomes a problem, in particular, when subjects are asked to think about a previously performed task, long after performance was under attention. A report of this type requires that the information-processing products be retrieved from memory and returned to attentional focus. It may not be as accurate as a similar report made at the time of processing, unless retrieval is able to completely recapture the initial contents of attentional focus.

The arguments of Ericsson and Simon are primarily directed toward establishing verbal reports as a valid psychological tool for accurate assessment of information processing. But it is also interesting to consider verbal reports under circumstances when they are not likely to be accurate: under conditions of retrospective report, extensive intermediate processing, or when many of the information-processing activities under question do not enter the conscious state. The fallibility of verbal reports under these circumstances has been emphasized by Nisbett and associates (Nisbett & Wilson, 1977; Nisbett & Ross, 1980), who examine the kinds of inference-making devices people use when introspecting about the underlying nature of their behavior. The particular behaviors they address go beyond the more basic information-processing activities that are of primary interest here, but their theoretical arguments are still important.

Examining the work of Ericsson and Simon and Nisbett et al., it would seem that we should distinguish between two senses in which verbal reports may be accurate or inaccurate. They may be accurate in that they validly describe information-processing activities that are supposed to be reported, or they may be accurate in the sense that they reflect what is consciously experienced, regardless of whether that experience derives from introspection, guesswork, or confabulation. Suppose we ask someone, (cf. Nisbett & Wilson, 1977) how she came to put her X in the upper right-hand corner of a tic-tac-toe game, and she says, "I was thinking of going across the top row." But suppose we also know from research that when people are presented with any three-by-three array of boxes and asked to make a mark, it is almost always placed in the upper right. We may then have our doubts about this person's "accuracy," in the first sense of the word. That is, we think her X was placed in the upper right because of a preference for that position that has nothing to do with tic-tac-toe. But on the other hand, this person may be "accurate," in the sense that she is reporting precisely what she is aware of as her reason for placing the X in the upper right.

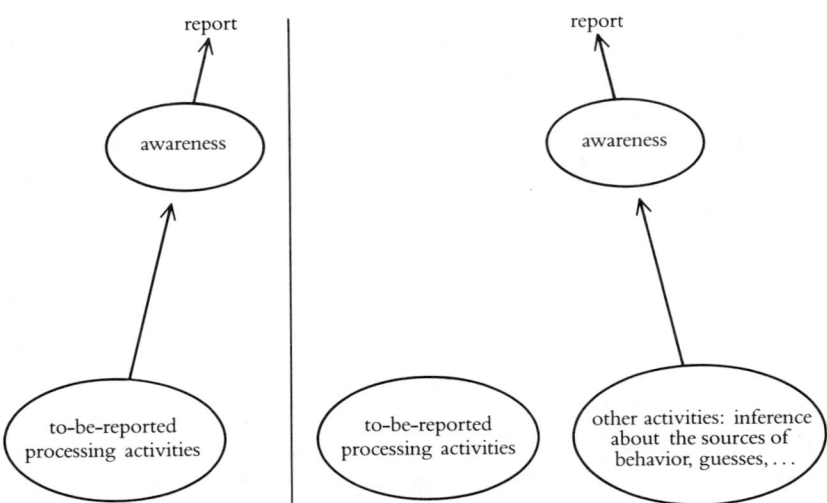

Figure 1.3   Two types of "accurate" verbal reports. Left panel reports reflect awareness of targeted activities; Right panel reports reflect awareness, but not of targeted activities.

These two senses of accuracy of verbal report are indicated in Figure 1.3. On the left, we see the first sense: what is reported is directly related to the information-processing activities that were supposed to be reported. On the right, we see the second sense: what is reported is what the reporter is aware of, although it is not really directly related to the processes of interest.

Both senses of the word "accuracy" are of interest, and for each there are potential problems with verbal reports. Relaxing the idea of what makes a verbal report accurate—so that one doesn't worry about whether it validly describes the information processing that led to an experience, but only whether it validly reports that experience—does not eliminate the problems. It is possible that the person who claims she was trying to complete the top row is inaccurate on both counts. She may be saying that because she thinks it is what the researcher want to hear, or she may be aware of another reason (like a position preference) but not want to report it. But on the other hand, the Ericsson/Simon model can be applied here: If our tic-tac-toe player can bring under attention what she thinks is her reason for placing the X, and it is translateable into words, she should be able to articulate it. At the point where she is aware of a reason, her task is like Ericsson and Simon's level 1 or 2 verbalization (see Figure 1.2); she has but to translate it into words and say it.

In summary, verbal descriptions of information-processing activities should be used, but with some caution. If one's purpose is to use verbalization to accurately assess underlying information-processing activities, one should have some understanding of the amount of intermediate, inferential processing that underlies a verbal report. This will provide warning signals when the report is unlikely to be a valid reflection of the mental activities of interest. Psychologists commonly accept verbal reports in the form of recalled words or "yes" and "no" responses. In doing so, they are assuming that these are essentially level-1 verbalizations (in the Ericsson and Simon sense); that is, they assume that people can name words they have recalled and articulate their positive and negative feelings as "yes" and "no," without introducing major errors. But even reports that are subject to more inference and other intermediate processing can be of use, especially when editing and confabulation are discouraged and the verbalizations are supplemented with other research tools.

When intermediate processes are used extensively (and erroneously) in producing verbal reports, those reports are still of interest (especially to researchers who study the fallibility of introspection). Even if we feel that a tic-tac-toe player put an X in the box because of a position preference, we may be interested in the internal processes that led her to believe she had a top-row strategy.

This extended discussion of introspective reports may have created an inflated impression of their importance. In fact, the study of awareness and memory, within the information-processing framework, uses many and varied research tools. Where free verbalizations are used, they are generally supplemented with experiments that directly test their implications. Other measures of awareness that are far less controversial than introspective reports are used, including response time and constrained verbal outputs, which can be assessed relative to controls that measure the effects of guessing and confabulation. Introspective reports themselves can be analyzed, their content measured in various ways, and these measures related to others. The chapters that follow should give some indication of the richness of the methods used to investigate on-line, epistemic, and personal-model forms of awareness.

Before discussing awareness of memory, some general depiction of memory per se seems in order. Chapter 2 provides an information-processing account of memory that is drawn from many sources (and undoubtedly agrees entirely with none). With this as background, Chapters 3 and 4 go on to deal with on-line awareness of perceptual, motoric, and memory-retrieval processes. Chapters 5 and 6 focus on epistemic awareness and personal models, respectively.

2

Memory: An Information-Processing Model

Human memory, viewed as an information processing system, takes in, modifies, stores, and acts on information. The information-processing approach is often said to liken human memory to a computer. Although other analogies are quite reasonable (for example, memory is also like a complex corporation), the computer metaphor is a good one, superior to a host of other analogies that might be (or actually have been) adopted. Memory has neither the fidelity nor nonselectivity of a videotape recorder, for example. Nor is it captured in metaphors like flypaper, A filing cabinet, or Pandora's infamous box (although all these might convey certain attributes of memory). The computer comparison is more apt.

Like a computer, human memory includes capacious storage, and previously stored information is applied when novel operations are performed. The rules for performing operations on information are part of the knowledge of computers—and human memory. Both are linked to output and input devices—printers and optical scanners in the computer, motor systems and sense organs in the human. However, there are critical differences between these two processing systems. One difference is their degree of fallibility. Computers can be expected to perform the same task in the same way, producing the same result each time, electronic bugs excepted. Ideally at least, they do not lose or intermingle information unless induced to do so. Human memory is not as well protected against such vagaries.

LONG-TERM MEMORY

As depicted in Figure 2.1, the major component of human memory is long-term memory, a storehouse for an individual's knowledge about the world and his or her experiences in it. This knowledge can be subdivided in various ways, some of which are depicted in the figure. In particular, psychologists have found it convenient to discriminate between concepts—knowledge about the nature of things, be they abstract like *justice* or concrete like *table*—and the linguistic labels for these concepts. Another distinction can be made between conceptual knowledge that is not tied to any particular sense (a table is used for eating and often made of wood)—and knowledge that is more closely tied to the senses (how one's own table looks from a particular perspective and distance). The extent to which conceptual and more sensory knowledge are different is a matter of much dispute (Klatzky, 1984).

Another type of knowledge is used to perform motor acts. When you drive a strange car, your repeated reaching for switches in the wrong spots tells you that there is some sort of movement pattern in your memory. At a more skilled level, a pianist may retain knowledge about the sequence of finger movements needed to perform Mozart's Sonata in B flat major, a shotputter knows the sequence of acts that put the shot, and so on. Finally, Figure 2.1 depicts rule-based knowledge, which indicates what consequences should be produced, given certain antecedent conditions. Entering into rules as antecedents or consequences are the concepts, sensory representations, and motor sequences described earlier.

The representations of knowledge (or knowledge "units") in memory are interconnected as if by pathways or "associations." As we shall see, a common conception about knowledge in long-term memory is that it is organized by these interconnections into hierarchical systems, in which a high-order unit of knowledge dominates several low-order units. The possible relations between high- and low-order units vary. One relationship that has been suggested is a "structural" one. The unit of knowledge representing "square" might dominate or control subunits designating right angles at various orientations. Similar to this is the whole/part relationship. The knowledge unit "face" might dominate subunits representing eyes, nose, and mouth (Palmer, 1975). The hierarchical relationship can also indicate category membership (Quillian, 1969). Thus the category "birds" might encompass units for specific exemplars, like robins and sparrows. (We will see several examples of hierarchical arrangements of knowledge below.)

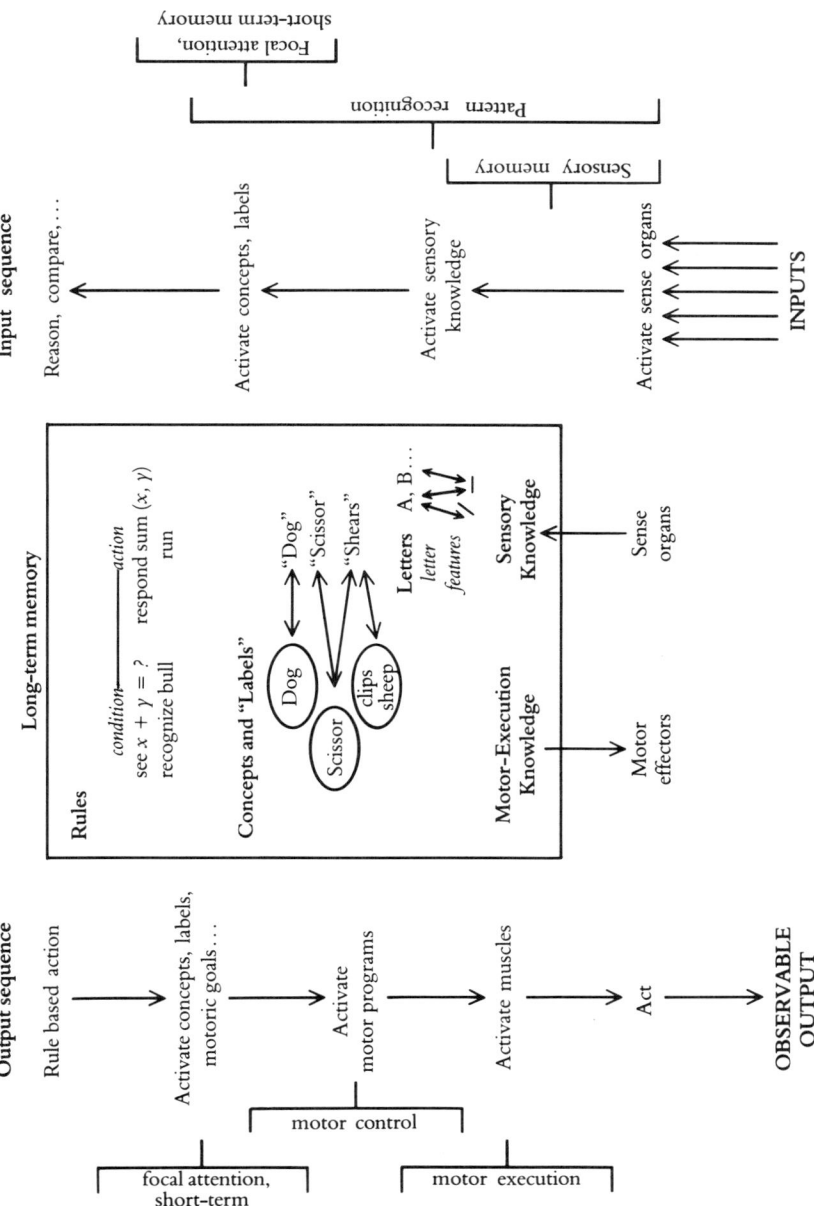

Figure 2.1 Depiction of the human memory system, including a store of sensory, motor, conceptual, verbal, and rule-based knowledge, and input and output processing avenues.

Another hierarchical organization can be imposed on knowledge in long-term memory, according to how directly it is related to the sense organs and motor effectors, so that knowledge units that are closely associated with the sensory and motor systems are placed low in the hierarchy, and more general conceptual knowledge is placed higher. The representation of a particular finger movement would be subordinate to knowledge that the movement is to be used to play the fourth note in a piano scale.

The pathways or associations in a hierarchy are not merely static connections. In theory, they are critical to the functioning, or processes, of the memory system. The act of perceiving (that is, apprehending the meaning of stimulation to the sense organs) can be described (at least in part) as a flow of activation or excitation along such pathways, from knowledge representations closely related to the sense organs to higher levels in a hierarchy. Executing a motor movement can be viewed as a sweep of excitation from high levels downward to knowledge representations that control motor output.

ATTENTION AND AUTOMATICITY

The representations of knowledge in long-term memory are formed, retrieved, and otherwise operated on by processes, which will be described further below. Processes activate and modify representations to produce perceptions, thoughts, and actions. A central idea in information-processing theories is that there is a limit to how many and what kind of processes can go on at the same time. This limit is called *attention*. The absence of a limit is *automaticity*. Attention-demanding (or attentional) processes are limited in their simultaneous application; automatic ones are not.

Over the course of the development of information-processing theories, the precise depiction of attention has changed. Early theorists (especially Broadbent, 1958) suggested that attention was some fixed site in the memory system that constituted a bottleneck or filter. Processes that were more peripheral (i.e., acted on knowledge representations located closer to the senses and motor effectors) were automatic; those applied after the bottleneck were restricted in their ability to co-occur.

The bottleneck idea was replaced by the depiction of attention as a limited capacity or resource pool from which processes draw, rather than a fixed location. There are several reasons for this change, an important one being that the same process seems to change in its demands, depending on the level of skill of the processor. Assuming that the location of the process in the information-processing system hasn't changed as skill develops (a tentative assumption, to be sure), it would seem that the location of attention must have changed. In any case, given this flexibility of application, it seems better to consider attention as capacity, which can be demanded by processes or not, depending on whether they are attentional or automatic.

The hallmark of an attention-demanding process is that its performance varies with other demands for attentional resources. In experiments, attentional demands can be manipulated by varying the complexity of a single task, or by causing several tasks to be performed. (The effects on performance will vary with how depleted the attentional pool is, among other considerations; Bobrow & Norman, 1975; Navon & Gopher, 1979). Consider a task in which a subject searches through briefly flashing arrays for a target letter, *M*. We measure the subject's performance by the time it takes him or her to spot an *M* and by the number of errors (misses of the *M* or false responses to some other letter). We now add another target letter, *S*, which the subject must look for along with *M*. If the task is attention-demanding, the subject's time and errors will increase. Shiffrin & Schneider (1977; Schneider & Shiffrin, 1977) have found just these effects for unskilled subjects. This example constitutes a case where demands on attention—as manipulated by the number of targets—are varied within a single task.

Another way to observe attentional demands experimentally is by requiring two tasks instead of one. In an early use of this technique, Posner and Boies (1971) asked subjects to perform a task of indicating whether two successive letters had the same name (*A* and *A* do; *A* and *a* do; *A* and *b* don't). The subjects also had to press a button whenever a noise signal occurred; this constituted a second task that might compete for processing capacity with the letter-matching task. Indeed, noise detection did appear to compete with letter matching. This was indicated by an increase in response time to the noise signal during the letter task, particularly when the signal was sounded just before the second letter occurred. Apparently, noise detection required capacity that was also needed for processes that anticipated the appearance of the second letter.

Automatic processes, in contrast to attentional ones, do not use attentional capacity. Thus they are unaffected by changes in the demands of the task that incorporates them or by the presence of another task. Some processes may be intrinsically automatic, but it also seems clear that attention-demanding processes can become automatized with the acquisition of skill. Consider, for example, the difference between a novice driver, entirely engrossed in controlling clutch, brake, and wheel, and a practiced driver, who holds a conversation while driving. For an experimental counterpart, Schneider and Shiffrin were able to show the development of automatization in the task described above, in which subjects searched for target letters in arrays of other distractor letters. The researchers reasoned that the subjects could become skilled at this task as long as they made a consistent "I detect" response to a letter. They could, in essence, practice detection of that letter. Following this reasoning, the researchers designated certain letters for skill development for each subject. These letters were assigned to a "consistent" set, so called because letters in that set never occurred unless they were targets on the current trial. Thus, if M was in the consistent set, it never occurred as a distractor in the flashing arrays when X was a target. M only occurred in the arrays when it was in the target set for the current trial and was to be detected.

Performance with this consistent set, after many (a couple of thousand) trials of practice, was compared both to performance early in the task, and to performance with another, "varied" set of letters after just as many trials. Letters in the varied set were used in such a way that detection couldn't be practiced. These letters were never consistently to be detected; a letter that was a target in one trial could be a distractor (and therefore to be ignored) in another.

The comparisons of performance suggested that automatization of detection occurred with members of the consistent set after many trials, but detection never became skilled with members of the varied set. The most important indication of automaticity was that the detection of consistent-set targets was eventually unaffected by task demands. Subjects could perform just as rapidly when several such letters were designated as targets as when there was only one such letter to detect in the current trial. In contrast, when the targets were from the varied set, the response time was longer and the error rate higher, the more targets were designated for a trial. This was the pattern even after many trials. This dependence of performance on task demands indicates that attention *was* being used for the varied-target detection. Subjects were also much slower with the varied-set targets; they actually took *longer* to do *worse* than with the consistent-set targets.

An important difference between attentional and automatic processes is the degree of willful control we have over them. Attentional processes can be controlled by the allocation of attention; we can follow instructions about what to attend to. For example, in early experiments by Cherry (1953), subjects were given two simultaneous auditory messages, one to each ear, and were told to attend to a particular ear. They were to "shadow"—repeat aloud—the attended message. The subjects showed they could shadow either of the two ears at will; they had no problem allocating attention. Their "problem" was that they could attend to only one of the messages; they could not report any of the content of the one they did not shadow.

Automatic processes, in contrast, are not under volitional control. They proceed even when we don't want them to. Subjects who had practiced in the Shiffrin/Schneider task with consistent targets could not avoid detecting them once they became skilled. The evidence for this comes from switching these subjects to a new task, in which they search for unpracticed (varied-set) letters that occur at two corners of a four-cornered square display. They are instructed to ignore items in the other two corners. However, when one of the to-be-ignored positions holds a letter from the consistently practiced set, detection of the unpracticed target in one of the other positions suffers. It seems that the practiced target is detected despite instructions to ignore its location. This automatic detection then captures attention-demanding processes, generating interference with detection of letters in other locations. Automatic detection cannot be inhibited on command.

MEMORY PROCESSES, INPUT AND OUTPUT

Alongside long-term memory in Figure 2.1 are some of the basic processes that operate on the knowledge in long-term memory. (The rules for performing these processes are presumably stored in long-term memory, so that memory is using itself to operate on itself.) Two avenues of processing are depicted, one proceeding from an external input, through the sense organs, to reasoning and thinking processes; the other originating in a rule and proceeding to the execution of some motor activity. (Although the avenues are spatially separated in the figure, this is not meant to indicate that they use entirely distinct knowledge representations, processes, or capacity; to the contrary, they may share many elements.) The first of these avenues has received far more research attention than the second and is thus the better articulated.

Sensory Processing and Pattern Recognition

The input avenue begins with a body of external stimulation impinging on the human organism. The sense organs that respond to this stimulation are receptive to inputs from many sources—odors, sounds, pressure and texture information from the skin, the muscular system, visual events. These inputs elicit activation, or excitement, in the sense organs and the pathways from them to the brain. This activation occurs at many levels—in the sense organs themselves, along various neural pathways that connect them to the brain, and within the brain itself. At some or all of these levels, the activation provides a sensory form of memory. That is, even after the stimulus at the sense organ has vanished, the activation may briefly persist, providing a "representation" of the stimulus even in its absence. In this sense, the activation is a form of remembering the stimulus, or at least its sensory properties. This sensory memory is to be distinguished from the larger body of sensory knowledge stored in long-term memory, which may or may not be active at any time.

The status of sensory memory in information-processing theories is currently under debate. One question is whether this kind of post-stimulus activation, which has been documented experimentally (Sperling, 1960; see reviews in Long, 1980; Coltheart, 1980), should be considered a form of memory. To the extent that the activation is in the sense organs or in the nerves leading directly from them, it does not seem very memory-like. Information-processing psychologists usually think of memory as something in the brain. Others have claimed that even if there is a sensory form of memory that briefly retains information about the physical aspects of a stimulus, it is not of much use to the activities of the information-processing system—perceiving, thinking, or remembering over longer intervals. (See, e.g., Haber, 1983.)

Whatever the status of sensory memory, the activation produced by external stimulation invokes a complex process called "pattern recognition." In general, this process draws a connection between current external stimulation (like a pattern of lines) and stored knowledge (like the form of letters). Attention plays a critical role here, because to some extent pattern recognition is a limited-capacity process.

At any one time, all of the sense organs are being stimulated and are therefore causing activation in the information-processing system (as indicated by the multiple arrows from "inputs" in Figure 2.1). But we cannot fully process what we are touching, hearing, smelling, tasting, and seeing, all at the same time. Recall that Cherry showed we can't even understand two different auditory messages at the same time. Thus at some point in this avenue of processing, the number of processed inputs must be considerably reduced. The information-processing system is said to *select* certain input sources, or "channels," for focal attention. These channels may undergo processing that uses some of the system's limited resources; other channels cannot.

Where does selection take place, and how much processing is received by channels that are not selected? In line with the general flexibility of attention, the answer to these questions varies from task to task and with skill (also from theorist to theorist). But even in studies with subjects who are not trained, it appears that many patterns simultaneously can receive enough processing so that they contact representations of their meanings in long-memory (as assumed by Deutsch & Deutsch, 1963; Norman, 1969). For example, a voice saying "cat" can contact sites in memory representing the concept cat, while another voice simultaneously saying "persimmon" also makes contact with persimmon-relevant sites. (Evidence for this will be presented in Chapter 3.) Because this initial contact can occur for many channels at once, it falls into the category of automatic processing. When one channel is selected, the related sites in long-term memory receive further processing with attentional capacity or focus.

As the passage above suggests, theories of pattern recognition often use the concept of activation to describe processing. In these theories, the early automatic stages of pattern recognition are treated as a modest degree of activation of sites in long-term memory. Attentional focus can also be described as activation, of a more selective sort. Thus there is early partial recognition (some activation) of many inputs, and later full recognition (focal attention and with it, more activation) of a limited set of inputs.

Pattern recognition models of this kind have been particularly well developed where the incoming stimuli are words, and recognition is essentially an early step in reading. Figure 2.2 depicts one such theory (McClelland & Rumelhart, 1982), which uses both the activation terminology and the concept of hierarchical representation. This theory assumes a hierarchy of knowledge about printed words which includes elements of distinct types at different levels. Each unit of knowledge is shown in the figure as a circular "node." At one level (bottom of Figure 2.2), the units correspond to visual features that make up letters, including vertical and horizontal lines at various heights. Above this level are nodes representing particular letters, and above them, each node represents a word. Connecting the nodes in this sytem are associations or pathways, along which "messages" may be passed from one node to another. The messages excite or inhibit activation at the receiving node.

At any point in time, each node may be in some state of activity: positive, inactive, or even inhibited. The level of activation depends in part on the frequency of occurrence of the stimulus that a node represents, as well as on the messages that it receives from other nodes. An excitatory

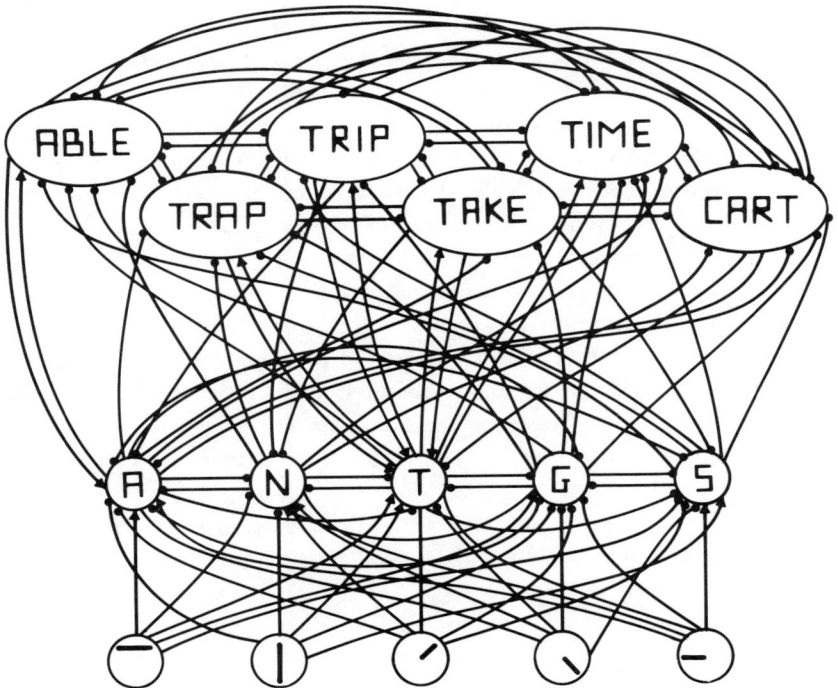

Figure 2.2   Pattern recognition model of McClelland & Rumelhart (1982), showing a three-level hierarchical representation and avenues of excitatory and inhibitory activation (denoted by arrows ending with points and dots, respectively).

message increases its activity; an inhibitory message depresses it. As a node becomes positively active, it sends messages to those nodes connected to it. Excitatory messages are sent to associated nodes that are consistent with the currently active node; for example, a featural node representing a horizontal bar would send an excitatory message to the letter-A node. Inhibitory messages are sent to nodes that are inconsistent with the currently active one; the horizontal bar would send an inhibitory message to the letter-N node.

The model assumes that nodes may become transiently active without producing recognition, but if sustained activity takes place in some node, the probability of the corresponding entity—feature, letter, or word—becoming reportable increases. This is what happens when a stimulus word is actually presented. The features in the input excite feature nodes, which in turn excite consistent letter nodes and inhibit inconsistent ones.

The excitation and inhibition is fed to word nodes, which generate their own messages if activated. In general, the word node that is consistent with the input will receive maximal excitation and minimal inhibition. Ultimately, it will be recognized and reported—at this point attentional capacity is tapped.

This whole process may receive excitation not only from the stimulus input, but also from the perceiver's expectations as to what might occur in the present context (Norman, 1969). This adds activation to the system from the top of the hierarchy, where conceptual ideas are located. For example, in a context where the perceiver has just read, "We sat around the kitchen," conceptual expectations would lead to the activation of the node for "table." This would excite letter and feature nodes representing the components of "table" and would inhibit other nodes, bringing the system to a faster resolution when "table" is actually presented. The flow of activation from the stimulus toward higher levels in the hierarchy is called "bottom-up" or "data-driven" processing; the flow from conceptual representations downward is called "top-down" or "conceptually driven" processing—for obvious reasons.

SHORT-TERM MEMORY

Past the point of recognition and selection in Figure 2.1 is short-term memory, more familiarly called STM. It has had various characterizations in its theoretical history, all of which are related. One way to conceive of STM is as a small storehouse or box for patterns that have recently been fully recognized. With the passage of time and/or additional recognitions, information once stored in STM passes out of the box. This version of STM is motivated in part by a well-known article of Miller (1956), who described a form of memory capable of holding about seven items or chunks of information. It was thought to be used in a "memory-span" task in which participants must repeat a brief list (e.g., of letters or digits) they have just heard. Using the STM-box concept, the scenario is as follows: Participant hears item, recognizes item, stores item in STM, does so for each item until told to recall, and regurgitates the items still in the box at the signal to recall.

Another view of STM subsumes the storage-box idea under the more general concept of a "working memory" (e.g., Baddeley, 1981). As this label suggests, STM is viewed as the site where mental work is performed. "Work" is any process that demands attentional capacity. This includes components of tasks like seeing an image in the mind's eye, adding sums "in the head," retaining a brief list of items like a phone number, or even comprehending speech and solving problems. Brief storage of information, as occurs in the memory-span task, can be seen as just another form of mental work. It is in fact necessary to mentally repeat or "juggle" a list of items to hold them for regurgitation; without such rehearsal the items are quickly lost (Muter, 1980; Peterson & Peterson, 1959). Thus, this brief STM storage, the "span," is effected by the work of rehearsal.

A directly related approach to STM is to associate it with attentional capacity: Giving focal attention to incoming information corresponds to storing the information in STM, and any other mental activity that uses attentional capacity takes place in STM. According to this view, once an item passes from attentional focus, it may remain in STM only briefly. To the extent that mental "work" is identified with attention, the idea that STM is attentional focus and that it is a working memory are very similar. The attentional view will be adopted here; that is, STM will be assumed to be a memory for information currently (or very recently) under attentional focus.

Motor Processing and Representation

The sequence of operations just described—from input to a sense organ, to capacity-demanding thinking and short-term storage—is but one avenue of processing that uses the knowledge in long-term memory. To the left of Figure 2.1 is depicted another avenue, corresponding to the generation of motor movements under the initiation of some rule. This can occur if we are following a rule like, "If you are in a game of darts, and the dart is in your hand, and your hand is behind your shoulder, throw your arm forward and release the dart." (Of course, motor movements may be initiated more directly, like the well known knee reflex.)

The concept of hierarchical representation is central to theories of motor control, as it is to theories of pattern recognition (Fowler & Turvey, 1978; Keele, 1981). Figure 2.3 illustrates a theory about the internal structures that control walking in a cat (after Gallistel, 1980; Weiss, 1941). These structures form a hierarchy of components which are assumed to communicate by excitatory and inhibitory messages when walking is implemented.

The figure represents a six-level hierarchy. At the first, lowest level, is a collection of nodes, each of which represents a motor unit—a neuron projecting to fibers in a muscle. Many such motor units feed into a single node at the next (second) level. This node represents a cluster of neurons that, if fired, are sufficient to produce a simple motoric contraction. At

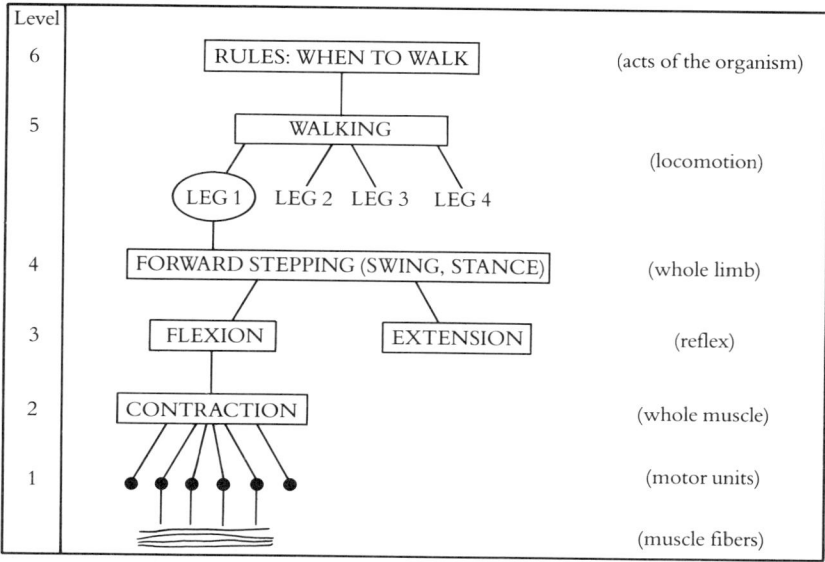

Figure 2.3   Hierarchical representation of the motor control system for walking in the cat.

the third level are simple reflex nodes, which control groups of muscular contractions that are used to accomplish a simple motor behavior. The behaviors of interest are flexion, which lifts the cat's leg off the ground, and extension, which puts it down. The fourth level has nodes that coordinate the reflexes in a whole limb and time them so as to execute a gait. For example, the cat needs a level-four node to control forward stepping. This alternately implements a swing phase, in which flexion is used and the foot lifts and advances, and a stance phase, when the leg is extended to support the cat. The legs are coordinated in a node at level five, which controls an entire gait. Finally, level six brings the walking system into a common node with other kinds of information. An example of this level is such rule-based knowledge as, "Walk forward if the light is white." The top of this hierarchy can be activated when the condition for the rule is satisfied, and by means of descending messages of excitation and inhibition that progress from level to level, the act of walking can be implemented.

A higher-level node in a hierarchical system like that just described, which coordinates simpler components, can be thought of as a motor "program." Like a program in a computer, it is an organized plan for performance. Sometimes these programs can be quite specific, like the program that coordinates the limbs of the salamander. When the front legs of a salamander are surgically reversed, the animal becomes incapable of locomoting (Weiss, 1941) because of a high-level control node that forces them into coordination with the rear legs. Signals for forward motion cause this node to direct the now reversed front legs backward while the rear legs still go forward. Uncoupling control of the pairs of legs to correct the problem appears to be impossible (Gallistel, 1980). The program runs off regardless of feedback about its inappropriateness; this very feedback independence has been posited to be a critical aspect of motor programs (Keele, 1968).

As we go higher in the evolutionary chain organisms are wired more flexibly, and programs appear to become less rigid. In fact, a common theme in theories of motor representation is that upper levels in the hierarchy do not fully specify muscular acts, but rather give general plans for action that can be potentially implemented in many ways (e.g., Schmidt, 1975). Lower levels in the system may not be entirely subordinate to upper ones, but may initiate behavioral control in their own right; for this reason the hierarchy is sometimes called a "heterarchy" (Newell, 1978; Turvey, 1977). We can see the generality of high-level motor nodes merely by observing that there are many ways to implement the same motoric result. We can write our name by controlling movements of the hand at the wrist or at the shoulder, and the results will be similar. Indeed, writing with the foot also gives a similar result (Raibert, 1977).

Schmidt (1975) and Pew (1974) have described highly generalized motor representations called motor schemas. These represent classes of actions which can be implemented by more specific versions as circumstances demand. For example, we might have a general ball-throwing schema, which is made more specific in accordance with the weight of the ball, distance it is to be thrown, and so on. Schmidt's schemas have two components. The "recall" portion gives sufficient information for the execution of a rapid movement, with minimal regard to feedback from the muscular system about its correctness. Only practiced movements have the fluidity and speed to be executed in this fashion, by the recall schema alone. The "recognition" component of the schema is used in slower actions; sensory feedback is monitored during the act of moving and is used to correct a motion while it is still in progress.

A Few Words about Thinking

If one avenue of processing goes from the senses into memory, and another goes from memory out to the active motor system, we might conceptualize "thinking" as a third avenue of processing that sends activation among high-level units in memory. Information-processing psychology has a lot to say about cognition, which it divides into subtopics like problem-solving, reasoning, and concept formation.

A general discussion of those topics goes far beyond the scope of this book. However, it is important to note that the study of memory is the study of thinking as well. Memory is critically important to the processes that are usually thought of as high-level, "cognitive" operations. And processes that are directly related to memory, such as acquiring new knowledge in long-term memory and retrieving it when needed, are very much like problem solving, reasoning, and concept formation. In other words, thinking involves memory, and memory involves thinking.

Theories of thinking incorporate assumptions about memory in a variety of ways. For one, long-term memory is assumed to hold the rules that are used for reasoning, forming concepts, and attempting to solve problems. It also holds critical information needed for these activities, such as the meanings of symbols (like $+$ and $=$) or exemplars of categories. Less obviously, short-term or working memory is also an important element in complex cognitive operations. Working memory is assumed to hold information that is immediately being used. Doing mental arithmetic requires storing place information and the results of intermediate computations for a short time. Chess players may use working memory to hold several possible moves, and their possible outcomes, when deciding which action is appropriate for the next turn. En route to forming a concept or solving a problem, thinkers must consider past hypotheses they have held and results of initial efforts; this requires working memory.

A particularly important role has been assigned to memory in certain theories of inference. According to Tversky and Kahneman (1971, 1973, 1974; Kahneman & Tversky, 1972, 1973), people are likely to make use of knowledge in memory, together with heuristics or general strategies for reasoning, when making certain kinds of inferences. Two important strategies are the "availability" and "representativeness" heuristics. The availability heuristic is used when people judge how frequent or likely events are. The heuristic says, in essence: determine how available or accessible the events are, and judge frequency by availability. The representativeness heuristic is used when determining how well new things fit into known categories. It says determine how well the attributes of the new thing match those of the known category, and judge membership in the category accordingly.

I will further discuss these heuristics in a later chapter. For the present it is important to note how heavily they make use of knowledge in long-term memory. One way to determine the availability of an object or event is to try to retrieve, from memory, instances involving it. If I ask you to tell me how frequently minor car accidents occur, you may try to think of instances in which you had one or observed one. Your ability to do so, the mental availability of car accidents, may underlie your judgment of their frequency. Similarly, representativeness judgments require knowledge in memory about the attributes of candidate categories into which new objects might be fit.

Many processes included in the topic of memory are also included in thinking, such as problem solving, reasoning, conceptualization, and the like. (This will be made clearly in the discussion of "remembering" that follows.) For example, suppose I ask you to remember what you did on your first date. It is possible that you remember this occasion very well and can simply state it. But for some people, this type of request initiates a process that is very much like solving a problem. You may approach it by trying to remember the age at which you were allowed to date, then recalling your place in school, then recalling names of candidates for dating who were with you in that school then. Or you may generate names of dates and try to order them in time. You may try to remember the types of dates you were allowed to have—group parties? movies?—and then attempt to recall specific occasions, ordered in time. Clearly, remembering is thinking.

REMEMBERING: ENCODING AND RETRIEVING

Under the general label of "remembering" are two important, complex types of activities: encoding, or adding new information to memory, and retrieval, getting at the encoded and stored information. In discussing these activities, we move away from a conception of the human information processing system as a fixed set of long-term memory representations, acted upon by processes. This discussion should make it clear that long-term memory is constantly being modified through experience.

In describing encoding and retrieval processes an important distinction is made between two kinds of knowledge in long-term memory: episodic and semantic (Tulving, 1972). Episodic knowledge concerns events of one's life; not only what happened but where and when, context as well as fact. Semantic knowledge is not tied to individual history; it is factual information that transcends a particular context. "Cats are chased by dogs" is a semantic fact; "my cat was chased by a dog yesterday" is an episodic fact.

Long-term memory acquires episodic knowledge by the occurrence of episodes of life. It is as if the pattern-recognition, working-memory, and motoric processes we have just described lay down "traces" in long-term memory. An episode in one's life changes the contents of memory, reflecting the sensory and conceptual aspects of what occurred. Not all sensory information that impinged on the organism is retained, and whatever information *is* retained is colored by the interpretations that were given it at the time. Episodic memory is more like an incomplete and embellished record of life than an exact copy. The embellishment and interpretation of experience, which shapes its ultimate representation in memory, is called "constructive processing." (As we shall see, just how much of episodic knowledge is "constructed" is a matter of debate.)

Semantic knowledge is derived from episodes. My belief that dogs chase cats is gleaned from many episodes—stories I read, dogs and cats I watched, anecdotes I was told. How semantic knowledge is derived from episodic encounters is unclear. It may take many episodes, varying in their contextual attributes, to create a semantic fact, but it may take only one. Children learn that one plus one makes two by many repetitions; they may learn that dogs bite by a single event.

Encoding into Long-Term Memory

"Encoding" is a term used to describe the process of acquiring both semantic and episodic knowledge. By "encoding" I mean subprocesses that perceive sources of new information, operate on the information using stored knowledge, and enter data (such as the perceived stimulation and records of operations) into memory. Some of these subprocesses are automatic; they do not require attention and proceed without voluntary control. For example, when I acquire information from a text, I begin with the recognition of printed patterns, much of which is automatic in a skilled reader. Other processes involved in encoding do use attention. Those mentioned in the previous discussion include "full" pattern recognition, short-term memory storage, and rehearsal.

It has been proposed by Hasher & Zacks (1979) that some episodic information is encoded into memory entirely by automatic processes, whereas other information requires attentional processing for its acquisition. (Actually, they assume a continuum of attentional demands, where fully automatic and attentional encoding processes would represent extremes.) The type of information that is encoded automatically appears to be different from that encoded attentionally; their ultimate memorability may differ as well as their content.

Everyday experience tells us that some information is encoded unintentionally. If we have a conversation with a friend, we may later remember where it took place, how the friend stood, what the friend was wearing, and other incidental details we had no intention of storing. These details seem to have been encoded without effort; their encoding may be automatic. Like other automatic processes, automatic encoding is assumed to be minimally modified by intention (even the intention to surpress it) and to be unaffected by capacity demands of other tasks occurring simultaneously. In addition, it is assumed to show minimal variation across individuals who vary in age, mental state, or practice—all of which could affect their pool of attentional capacity (Hasher & Zacks, 1979).

Attentional encoding is so called because it demands attention; it incorporates some form of mental work. Some types of work are more effective encoding devices than others; that is, they establish more retrievable knowledge in long-term memory. In general, mental work that is used to encode episodic events, such as the occurrence of a list of words that is later to be remembered, is more effective when it relates the new, to-be-encoded information to existing conceptual information in long-term memory. When encoding a list of words in preparation for a "free recall" test (reporting the words in any order), it is more effective to think about the meaning of each as it occurs than to think about whether it is in capital or lower-case letters (Craik & Tulving, 1975). An attentional encoding device that will be discussed in a later chapter is thinking about the meanings of to-be-remembered items in relation to one another; for example, trying to relate words on a list by weaving a story around them.

On the other hand, it is impossible to say what an effective means of encoding is unless we know in what situation the information is to be retrieved. Suppose the retrieval situation is a test on information that is assumed to be automatically encoded. One such type of information is the frequency with which a repeated event has occurred (Hasher & Zacks, 1979). We can test memory for frequency by presenting some stimulus and asking how often it occurred in the past. For example, subjects can study a list in which different words are presented with different frequencies, then be shown each of the words and asked for its presentation frequency. If frequency *is* encoded automatically, their ability to retrieve this frequency information should be unaffected by their voluntary, effortful activities at the time the original stimuli were presented. (This has in fact been found—Hasher & Zacks, 1979.) There will be no best way to encode this sort of information voluntarily, if voluntary activities of all kinds are ineffective.

Even if we restrict our memory tests to information that is thought to be encoded with effort, the type of test may be critical to determining the most effective encoding device. Consider the situation in which subjects encode a list of words. Thinking about the meaning of each word will be best if the test calls for free recall, in which retrieval of meaning is assumed to be very important (e.g., Craik & Tulving, 1975). Similarly, the weaving-into-a-story technique will aid free recall because retrieval of its general plot can be used to trigger retrieval of individual words. However, thinking about a word's *appearance* rather than meaning may be the best way to encode information for a test in which a previously seen word is shown, and one is asked whether the word is in the same or a different typeface from its initial presentation (as in *"PERSIMMON: Was it originally printed in capitals or lower case?"* cf. Morris, Bransford, & Franks, 1977).

Retrieval

The foregoing considerations should make clear that remembering depends on more than encoding. It requires that previously encoded information, stored as a knowledge representation in long-term memory, be retrieved from storage. Theories of retrieval generally divide the process into several components. These include cue generation, memory search, and decision. An act of retrieval begins with some sort of cue, which may be general or specific. We may be asked, for example, to remember all of the countries south of the U.S. border in North and South America. This is a general retrieval cue that is likely to elicit "Mexico" as a first response. A more specific retrieval cue for Mexico is, "A country that shares borders with Texas"; an even more specific cue, one which looks a lot like what is to be retrieved (but is nevertheless better thought of as a cue), is "Mexico" (i.e. the cue "Mexico" elicits the response "Mexico").

Cues give some sort of access to memory, which can be said to initiate a search for the cued representation. A very general cue is likely to require more subsequent search than a specific one, although that isn't necessarily the case. "A country south of the U.S." looks like a very general cue and "Mexi—" like a specific one, but Mexico is so prominent an exemplar of this category that little search for its representation in memory is needed, and the general cue might be as effective as the name cue. On the other hand, "Guatema—" is probably going to be a much more efficient cue for the memory representation of that nation than "A Central American country."

The decision component of retrieval is used to determine whether accessed information is indeed what was specified by the initial cue. In retrieving countries, for example, I might pick up "Bogotá," which requires a bit of decision effort. Is Bogotá a country in Central or South America? Many of the right associations are there, but ultimately I decide that it is not, because I have also retrieved, in association with Bogotá, the fact that it is the capital of Colombia.

A fourth component that can be included in retrieval is "response generation." When subjects must report words, in particular, they must generate those words from what has been retrieved, which may not be very wordlike. For example, in my search for countries, I might have a strong visual image of one in the upper right corner of South America, above Brazil, but not be able to generate its name. I have retrieved the country in some sense, but will still be in error in the sense of not producing the appropriate response.

Retrieval can be very rapid in some cases, very laborious in others. The process of recognizing a familiar pattern, such as a cat or the word *cat*, is a form of retrieval, in that it provides access to knowledge in memory through some retrieval cue (the recognized stimulus). This kind of retrieval is rapid and largely automatic. On the other hand, if I try to remember names of high school classmates, I may go through a rather laborious effort. This latter type of retrieval may involve a cyclic alternation between cue generation and search, in which what I retrieve at one point (a member of the choir) provides a cue that enables me to successfully search for other information (other choir members). I will have more to say about automatic and effortful retrieval in Chapter 4.

AWARENESS AND THE GENERAL MODEL

This extended general discussion of the information-processing approach to human memory has several purposes. Most important, I hope that it has established that the present focus is on awareness in the specific context of contemporary memory theories. The topic of awareness is obviously of interest in many diverse contexts, but the psychology of human memory is a particularly interesting one. Theories of memory are making increasing use of the construct of awareness, and there is a body of empirical phenomena that, I believe, establishes awareness as a legitimate substantive topic within memory.

Chapter 1 suggested that there are several manifestations of awareness of memory, and the present overview is intended to provide a general framework for their interpretation. To reiterate, there are on-line awareness, epistemic awareness, and personal memory models.

On-line awareness was described as conscious experience of ongoing information-processing activities. As I have indicated, it will be assumed that its counterpart in memory theory is attention (or short-term memory). (A direct relationship between awareness and attention will be assumed, but it is not claimed that the two are synonymous.) The implications of this assumption for perceptual performance, memory retrieval, and skills will be explored in the two chapters that follow.

Epistemic awareness is cognizance of the contents of one's memory. From the present chapter, this can be viewed as an outcome of a complex process that is a component of "remembering," which incorporates encoding as well as retrieval. Chapter 5 will more extensively describe epistemic awareness as deriving from cued searches for previously encoded information and decision processes that act on what is retrieved.

Personal memory models, the third general type of awareness, comprise beliefs about the general nature of memory and about oneself. The content of these beliefs and their potential sources are the focus of Chapter 6. Beliefs about memory may be imparted directly; they may be inferences from publicized events; they may be synthesized from many past and highly personal experiences. The beliefs that constitute personal memory models may be valid or invalid, leading to another reason for the extended discussion of the present chapter: It provides a set of psychological beliefs against which the validity of folk knowledge can be assessed.

3

On-Line Awareness

In computer jargon, "on-line" refers to interactions that are direct and reasonably immediate, such as those that occur when a user types commands at a terminal. Someone who punches cards and brings them to a computer center is not on line. By on-line awareness, I mean monitoring of the here and now in a direct, immediate fashion; awareness of ongoing internal processes and, through them, of external events. This chapter concerns not only such awareness, but equally important, its absence.

As Chapter 1 indicated, "on–line awareness" is essentially conscious experience—within the restricted focus of information-processing theories of memory. But what does it gain us to relate these theories to consciousness, beyond providing a new name for an experience that has been analyzed, speculated about, and reinterpreted for centuries? There are several ways to answer this question. One approach, which I have *not* taken here, is to use information-processing notions to theoretically account for the experience of consciousness. (See Marcel, 1983b, for an important theory.) An alternative to applying information processing to consciousness is to apply consciousness to information processing; for example, to add to models of memory a theoretical component called "conscious experience." (This approach is discussed in Carr, 1979; Underwood, 1979.) However, the role that might be played by this addition is unclear; it seems that it would overlap considerably with the existing components called "working memory" and "attention," as described in Chapter 2. So again, this is not the approach taken here. What I *have* chosen to attempt in this chapter is a compromise. I assume as a starting point that on-line awareness is directly related to the information-processing concept of attentional capacity. I then explore certain implications of that assumption. In so doing, I consider two common beliefs about awareness (or its absence) and behavior: one concerns sensory experience, the other, skilled performance. These beliefs are, stated simply, that our behavior is affected by stimulation that we are unaware of perceiving, and that consciously experiencing a practiced activity somehow interferes with it. Setting these beliefs in information-processing terms enables us to understand when and why they may be true. Symbiotically, this same effort makes more explicit the role of on-line awareness in information processing; thus it is a vehicle for expanding theories of memory, perception, and peformance.

ON-LINE AWARENESS AND ATTENTION

In his classic book *Principles of Psychology* (1890, Chap. 16), William James drew a connection between consciousness and what he called primary memory, which is essentially what we are calling short-term memory.

To James, primary memory was the store for just perceived and apprehended stimulation, and consciousness of this stimulation was composed of its "after-memory," influenced by knowledge brought to bear in perceiving and comprehending it. Objects stored in long-term (or what James called secondary) memory could also be brought into consciousness; "revived anew" by the act of recollection. If we assume, as discussed in Chapter 2, that short-term memory holds the information currently attended to, we could elaborate James's view to say that elements of the information-processing system become conscious to the extent that they receive attentional activation.

To expand on this idea, recall from Chapter 2 that a distinction is made between two types of activation, or two types of processes, within the memory system: automatic and attentional. Automatic processes do not make demands on the limited capacity of the information-processing system and thus do not interfere with other processes that do. Attentional processes do demand capacity, and they occur only at the cost of a diminished ability to perform other capacity-demanding processes. Attentional processes are under volitional control and respond to instructions; automatic processes cannot be controlled at will, or even inhibited. Automatic processes include those that occur very early in perception; attentional processes are relatively late. Attentional processes tend to be slow; automatic ones tend to be fast. Automatic processing tends to characterize skills; attention is devoted to what is novel and unpracticed. Most important, it will be assumed here that automatic processes are characterized by a lack of awareness and that awareness reflects the use of attentional capacity.

The idea that awareness (for the rest of this chapter, I will generally omit "on-line") is directly related to attention is a common one in information-processing theories (see especially Ericsson & Simon, 1980; Mandler, 1975; Marcel, 1980; Posner, 1978; Shallice, 1978). Posner and Klein (1971) cited several aspects of attentional capacity that seem also to be characteristic of awareness. One is the lateness of its occurrence in perception; attention is assumed to be invoked after substantial sensory processing. We would similarly expect awareness to be related to processes that occur centrally, away from the sensory periphery. Awareness is not a property of the sense organs, but of their interpreters. Moreover, attentional capacity can be applied flexibly and selectively; awareness shares this flexibility.

Although it has been commonly expressed that awareness is related to the concept of attention, the nature of the relationship is considerably less explicit. One possibility is that we derive awareness by executing specific attention-demanding processes, which operate just for this purpose (cf. Marcel, 1983b). (This suggests that some processes that require attention might not produce awareness.) Another possibility is that awareness is a byproduct of any process that uses attention. Yet another possibility is that awareness is quite independent of attention (as defined in information-processing models) but they just happen to share attributes like volitional control and limited capacity. Under these latter assumptions, awareness need not have any particular function in information processing; it could be an epiphenomenon. At the risk of being "gingerly and skitterish," Mandler's (1975, p. 44) terms for contemporary psychologists' dealings with consciousness, I am not going to adopt any of these particular assumptions about the relationship between attention and on-line awareness. I will take the more general view that awareness is associated with the expenditure of attention, and not with automatic processes.

An attempt to draw even this loose a connection between attention and awareness is not unequivocally accepted; even the more basic distinction between attentional and automatic processes has its detractors (e.g., Hirst, Spelke, Reaves, Caharack, & Neisser, 1980; Kinsbourne, 1981; Ryan, 1983). In fact, these simple dichotomies are undoubtedly too simple. The contribution of attention to a process is a matter of degree—and so too may be awareness.

A specific problem that has been raised with the attention/awareness connection is that certain information-processing activities, thought to be "high-level" in the hierarchy of memory functions, or "central" rather than "peripheral," and that might be thought to demand attentional capacity on just that basis, can be performed without awareness. For example, Hirst et al. (1980) asked subjects to write down dictated sentences while reading an unrelated text. After lengthy practice over a period of weeks, some subjects could take the dictation without a loss in reading speed or comprehension of the text. Not only could they write the dictated sentences, they showed they could extract and integrate their meanings. For example, after having received the dictated sentences "Their house burned. Everything was destroyed. Firemen arrived late," they were likely to feel that a sentence implied by these sentences ("Everything was burned") was familiar. Drawing implications from dictated sentences is a high-level, "central" cognitive activity. Yet, the subjects reported that they were unaware of the meaningful relations among successive sentences as they were dictated, and unaware of having integrated them. On this basis it appears that this high-level activity was performed without awareness. As Hirst's study points out, we must not confuse the claim that *low*-level processing is likely to be automatic with the claim that *high*-level processing is likely to be attentional. Flexibility of attentional control may apply both to abstract thought and peripheral processing (although it may be harder to automate nonperipheral processes).

The assumption that awareness is associated with attentional processing, its detractors notwithstanding, offers certain insights into both memory and awareness. The purpose of the remainder of this chapter is to explore these insights by adopting this assumption, together with the framework of the information-processing approach. We can then consider what information-processing theories have to offer in furthering our understanding of awareness, and what the study of awareness tells us about information processing and memory.

An important feature of the information-processing model is that it links awareness to unskilled behaviors. A lack of attentional demands, or automaticity, appears to characterize information-processing skills, whether they involve perceptual and motor systems or higher thought processes. At least some information-processing activities that make attentional demands when novel make fewer demands when well practiced. Given the assumed close relationship to attention, then, we would expect awareness to be associated with what is infrequent and unhabitual rather than what is familiar and skilled.

Another contribution of the information-processing model is to differentiate among avenues of processing within which skills might develop. One area of potential development is along the input or perceptual pathway, which includes early sensory activation and pattern recognition. As we will see, the recognition of objects and words is (in literate people, at least) an activity with automatic components. Another avenue of information-processing activities culminates in observable output, a performance. I include here motor performance and outputs in other domains, such as solutions to problems. Again, these are areas where skills appear to develop with practice. Earlier I mentioned two common beliefs about awareness that can be reexamined fruitfully from the information-processing perspective: that there are sensory experiences that affect our behavior without our being aware of it, and that awareness is debilitating to skilled performance. It is apparent that these beliefs map onto the two information-processing pathways, input and output.

As Chapter 1 indicated, a critical question in the study of awareness is how to evaluate it with some observable measure. In the case of the perceptual pathway, a measure of awareness is not difficult to find. One can assume that a perceptual activity has culminated in awareness if it can be reported in some reasonably direct way, such as with a verbal label or a statement that equates a new stimulus with a previously perceived pattern. It is harder to determine awareness of a performance, which produces some primary output that is not directly related to awareness. If the performance is motoric, the achievement of movements does not indicate the mover is aware of their production. We are obviously unaware of many daily motor acts, from habitual lip smacking or hair pulling to driving a car along a familiar route. In this domain, then, we must consider ad hoc verbalizations as indications of on-line awareness of performing.

It is important not only to find measures of awareness, but to find behavioral measures of mental activities of which we are unaware. This turns out to be easier in the performance domain, where there is an observable output not tied to awareness, than in the perceptual domain. Nonetheless such measures are available and make it possible to consider the automatic as well as attentional components of information-processing and to relate them to skill level.

ON-LINE AWARENESS AND THE PERCEPTUAL PATHWAY

The present section will examine skilled pattern recognition as it occurs in reading and categorization of common objects. We will examine not only perceptual activities of which we have conscious experience, but those of which we do not. Our concern will be with what might be called the awareness boundary. There appear to be components of perception that fall on both sides of this boundary, and we can better understand why, by considering such information-processing constructs as attention/automaticity and hierarchical structure.

Perceptual Skills

At the outset I will need some justification of the claim that pattern recognition of words and objects is a skilled activity; that it has automatic components. The rest of the chapter provides a variety of evidence on this point, But for now consider a rather compelling demonstration of the automaticity of object and word recognition, indicating that we cannot willfully prevent its occurrence. In the case of words, the demonstration was provided by Stroop in 1935. He asked subjects to name the color of ink in which words were printed and measured their naming time. When the words were themselves the names of other colors (for example, *blue* was printed in orange ink, and thus the correct response was "orange"), color-naming times increased, relative to those required for neutral words (*book* printed in orange, for example). This occurs despite concerted efforts by the subjects to avoid it. (You can easily try this test for yourself.) The reading of the word is automatic; it cannot be eliminated; and it interferes with naming the ink color.

There has been much work on the Stroop phenomenon, including some that has extended it to pictures of objects. It seems that in general, you can produce the phenomenon by finding a fast process, initiated automatically, that competes for responses (internal or overt) with a slower process. The speed of the former means it will generate a response first and thus win the competition; the automaticity of this same process means that it can't be inhibited and prevented from impeding the second process. In the case of perceiving objects, this situation is fulfilled by the following task (Smith & Magee, 1980): Subjects are shown a picture (e.g., a frog) with a name on it ("scarf"). They are asked to categorize the word (say whether it is clothing, for example), a task which has often been found to be slower than categorizing a picture (Faulconer & Potter, 1975; Guenther, Klatzky, & Putnam, 1980). In this situation, the presence of the picture from another category interferes with and slows the categorical response to the word, even though subjects are instructed to ignore the picture. This inability to inhibit interfering processes indicates that the picture automatically accesses related category information in long-term memory.

Note that in the examples I have given, the process does not proceed entirely without attention. The fact that recognizing one pattern interferes with responses to another stimulus indicates that the processing of the first pattern is, at some stage, using attention. But this use of attention seems to begin relatively late in recognition, after the stimulus has made contact with a meaningful representation in memory (see Glaser & Glaser,

1982). The earlier components of recognition appear to be automatic, as evidenced by their resistance to being inhibited. As in the Shiffrin/Schneider studies described in Chapter 2, captured attention is a consequence of automatic activation.

Given the assumption that awareness goes with attention, it appears that much of the recognition process will proceed without awareness for these automatically recognized kinds of stimuli, although the final recognition response is experienced. It may not come as a surprise that some studies appear to eliminate this ultimate full-recognition response, so that only the automatic components of recognition remain. This phenomenon has been called "subliminal" or "unconscious" perception. It is the experimental version of the common belief that we are affected by stimuli that we are unaware of perceiving.

Subliminal Perception: Early Work

Research on perception without awareness has a rather fractious history, as reviews by Dixon (1971, 1981), Erdelyi (1974), and Shevrin and Dickman (1980) make clear. In essence, the phenomenon is a simple one: a stimulus that fails to produce an overt recognition response (such as "I saw an X"), despite concerted efforts by the stimulus presenter to elicit that response, nevertheless produces other effects, such as better-than-chance "guessing" about the stimulus's identity. Acceptance of such phenomena as real requires a straightforward psychological assumption (Blum, 1961; Dixon, 1971; Erdelyi, 1974); that all behavioral responses to a stimulus are not linked to its full recognition and conscious identification, but rather, that some responses can be produced without incurring awareness of identification.

There has been considerable unwillingness to accept this assumption in the scientific community. Dixon (1971) suggests that one reason for this is the fear that subliminal perception is unscientific, even romantic or mystical. This fear may in turn stem from an emphasis on behavioral measurements in psychology. The very notion that there are important behaviors that cannot be consciously apprehended or observed was enough to make some experimentalists shudder. Since conscious apprehension is essential to so many behavioral measures, it raises the possibility that psychological methods will miss some of the most critical mental phenomena. Then, too, perception without awareness appeared to create a link between "scientific" and "Freudian" psychology, anathema to many scientists.

Another source of scientific resistance (Dixon, 1971) is the seemingly irrational quality of the phenomenon. Consider one manifestation, called "perceptual defense" (reviewed in Brown, 1961; Dixon, 1971, 1981; Erdelyi, 1974), which is a lowered ability to perceive emotion-laden stimuli relative to innocuous ones. In early work this defense was manifested as a need for a longer presentation time in order to perceive "taboo" words than was needed for inoffensive words. The phenomenon was seemingly inexplicable to those who read early reports. How could perceivers defend themselves against emotional words, rendering themselves incapable of perceiving, when they had not yet perceived the words?

Alternative explanations of the phenomenon were offered in order to avoid the idea that subliminal perception existed. For example, it was argued that emotion-laden words were less frequent in natural discourse and less perceptible for that reason. Or it was argued that subjects were reluctant to speak the taboo words, even if they had perceived them, so that they resisted until a sufficiently long presentation made it clear that the words must have been identified. Similar counterexplanations were offered for other findings that seemed to indicate perception without awareness.

Scientists reserve for certain seemingly unscientific phenomena a particularly great measure of skepticism. Even in the face of this, however, there is increasing acceptance of the validity of perception without on-line awareness. There are at least three reasons for this trend: (1) More sophisticated experiments (described below), which rule out many of the counterarguments and alternative explanations proposed previously, have made a more convincing case for the phenomenon. (2) These same experiments have provided a methodology which promises to bring these seemingly unmeasurable, "nonbehavioral" events under control, rendering them susceptible to experimental investigation. (3) Information-processing theories of perception have provided a coherent context and account of these phenomena, so that they no longer seem illogical or magical (Blum, 1961; Erdelyi, 1974).

As an example of more sophisticated methodology used to study the perception of emotional stimuli, consider an experiment by Erdelyi and Appelbaum (1973). The stimuli were emotionally neutral pictures, arranged in a circle around a center item that was either innocuous (a window) or emotional (a star of David or a swastika—the subjects were members of a Jewish organization). The arrays were flashed for under ¼ sec, and the viewers' ability to perceive them was measured by asking them to pick out the pictures on a test. Note that this use of neutral pictures eliminates the criticism that subjects are biased not to respond (as with taboo words). It also allows the same items to be reported in the emotional (swastika; star) and nonemotional (window) conditions, thus eliminating the claim that the defended-against stimuli differ from the others on dimensions like frequency. Still, evidence for suppression of perception was obtained: A measure of perceptual detectability was less with the emotional center than with the neutral one.

There have been a variety of experimental phenomena, in addition to perceptual defense, that have been taken as evidence for perception without awareness (see Dixon, 1971, 1981; Shevrin & Dickman, 1980). Some researchers (Corteen & Wood, 1972; Moray, 1970) used, as their measure of perception, electrical responses on the skin. Subjects in these studies performed in a dichotic listening task, in which they shadowed (repeated aloud) one of two messages that were presented simultaneously, one to each ear. As is typical in these tasks, subjects seemed to be quite unaware of the meaning of the unshadowed message. Yet, when it contained an emotional word, or one that had been paired with shocks earlier in the experiment, there was a skin response. In later studies, Dawson and Schell (1982) offered further support for this phenomenon using more stringent controls for switching attention between the ears.

Subliminal Perception: Recent Developments

Based on the concept of memory activation, a relatively new approach uses a "priming" paradigm to indicate perceptual processing without awareness. "Priming" refers to the following phenomenon: If two items (words, pictures) are presented in close succession (from milliseconds to seconds) and a response is required to the second item, the time for that response will be shorter when the items are related than when they are not. For example, the time it takes to say that "chair" is a word is less when *table* has preceded it than when *bread* has preceded it (Meyer & Schvaneveldt, 1971). More interesting for present purposes is evidence, first described by Marcel (1974), that this kind of priming effect can be found even when subjects are unaware of perceiving the first item.

The general procedure used to study priming without awareness, as devised by Marcel, includes two phases. First, each stimulus that is to be used as a prime (that is, as the first of the two items in a sequence) is briefly presented to the subject and followed by a "masking" display that impairs identification performance. The duration of the stimulus or the interval between that stimulus and the mask is manipulated, in an effort to find a critical presentation interval where the stimulus just fails to be identified. The goal is to find a critical value such that at longer intervals, the stimulus can be identified, and shorter intervals are not needed in order to guarantee nonidentification. In the second phase of these studies, the priming procedure described above is used, with the prime presented at this critical value (along with other comparison values), in order to determine whether the prime's occurrence can influence the processing of a subsequent item even when the prime itself cannot be seen.

In one experiment (McCauley, Parmelee, Sperber, & Carr, 1980; Experiment 2) subjects were asked to produce a name for one picture that had been briefly preceded by another picture, the prime. In the first phase of the study, two durations were established for each picture to be used as a prime. The "full threshold" was the minimum exposure time (in a procedure where the picture was presented, then followed by a masking stimulus made of fragmented and whole letters) that produced 100% accurate identifications over a six-trial series. (The mean for this threshold was 90 msec.) A "zero threshold" was 5 msec below the longest exposure time that produced zero identifications in a six-trial series. (The mean for this threshold was 53 msec.) During the next phase of the study, the subjects took part in a series of trials, during each of which they named a picture that had been preceded 500 msec earlier by a prime picture. The prime was presented for durations from above the full threshold to below the zero threshold—as low as ⅓ of its value. In some trials the prime was related to the second, named picture (as in a cat-dog sequence); in others it was unrelated.

The results of these studies were quite clear, as Figure 3.1 shows. When the exposure duration of the prime was as low as ⅔ the zero threshold value, the priming effect (defined as the reduction in naming time for the second stimulus when the first was related to it, as compared to unrelated) was 30 msec—even though none of the primes was identified at such a low exposure duration. In comparison, the effect of related primes exposed at the full threshold was 33 msec, not significantly different from the 30-msec value. Thus, a prime presented at a duration meant to preclude awareness had as profound an influence on subsequent processing as one that was fully recognized.

Experiments by Fowler, Wolford, Slade, and Tassinary (1981) and by Marcel (1980; 1983a, b; Marcel & Patterson, 1978) show similar priming effects with words. In research of Fowler et al. (Experiments 5 and 6), which was based on Marcel's earlier work, the effects of two kinds of word primes were compared—those presented for 10 msec and followed shortly after by a mask, and those presented for 500 msec and unmasked. The latter were easily seen. However, in the first condition, the duration of the period between prime and mask was adjusted to a point where subjects were at chance (guessing) levels in indicating whether any prime word at all (as opposed to a blank field) had been presented. The subject's

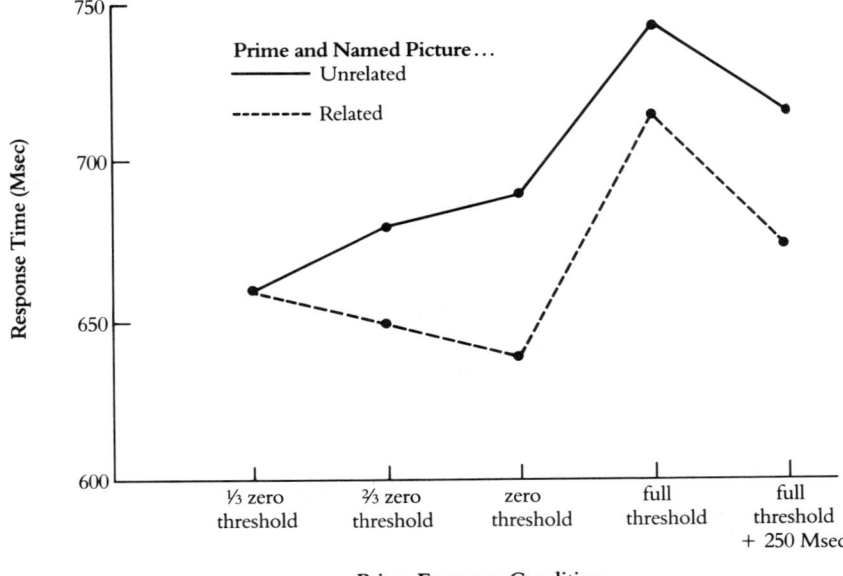

Figure 3.1   Time to name a picture as a function of the exposure time of the preceding picture (the prime) and the relatedness between the two pictures (From McCauley, Parmelee, Sperber, & Carr, 1980).

task during the experimental trials was to indicate whether the second of the two stimuli was a word or a nonword string of letters.

Again, priming effects were very similar, whether subjects could identify the prime word or whether it was presented so briefly that they apparently could only guess whether a word had been presented at all. When the first word was related to the second, response time to the second decreased, even though subjects reported not seeing the first word.

These studies attempt to demonstrate that automatic perceptual processing can influence behavioral measures, while remaining outside of awareness. Not everyone is convinced, however; there is still skepticism and methodological criticism. Merikle (1982) raised important questions about the adequacy of the procedures used in the initial phases of these studies, which attempted to guarantee that prime stimuli did not enter awareness. Indeed, relatively few trials were used in attempting to establish that primes could not be seen. Another problem, concerning differences in subjects' adaptation to light during the two phases of the procedure (finding the threshold versus the priming trials), has also been raised (Purcell, Stewart, & Stanovich, 1983).

Marcel (1983a, footnote 4) has reported some failures to replicate the priming-without-awareness results, but he also emphasizes that the phenomenon is quite vulnerable to small experimental variations, if these prevent critical perceptual processes from being executed. On the positive side, there has been replication of the priming effect, using more extensive procedures to establish the critical presentation conditions that preclude awareness (Balota, 1983). It should also be pointed out that the critical durations used by Fowler et al. were meant not merely to preclude identifying the words shown, but to eliminate awareness of whether a word had been presented at all (as opposed to a blank field). These durations should be below those needed for not only knowing a word occurred, but also identifying it. Moreover, MacCauley et al. found priming effects when primes were presented at ⅔ the value of the zero-identification threshold. So while the phenomenon seems destined to remain controversial for some time, it is not to be summarily dismissed.

The Pattern Recognition Model and Perception Without Awareness

As mentioned above, one reason for a greater tendency to accept the possibility of unconscious perception is a better understanding of how it can occur. The pattern recognition model of Chapter 2 tempts one to wonder how there could be any objection to the idea of perceptual influences on behavior without awareness. Before continuing, we should review the model: At any point in time, there are many sources or channels of information from the senses impinging on the information processor. Most or all of this information automatically activates related representations in memory; the degree of such activation depends on how frequently this same or similar stimulation has occurred before. Only limited sources of information can be selected for attention. The additional activation that accrues to representations of stimuli on an attended channel leads to their full recognition. Whether a channel is selected for attention depends on the perceiver's desires and expectations. Selection may also be triggered by high levels of automatic activation from information on some channel.

The key to the information-processing explanation of perception without awareness is the assumption that perception is a multilevel phenomenon rather than a simple event that either succeeds or fails. Conscious identification is treated as but one stage in perceptual processing, and rather a late one at that (Look at all the activational flow that precedes the final recognition response in the Rumelhart/McClelland model of Chapter 2.) In this fashion, the information-processing model fits the proposals of Dixon (1971) and Erdelyi (1974), which state that any account of subliminal perception must unlink perceptual responses to stimuli from on-line awareness; a theory of subliminal perception must allow for the idea that an identification response is but one possible measurable outcome of perceptual processing.

Consider perceptual defense from the information-processing perspective. The defense against a taboo stimulus can be assumed to take place after it has aroused a certain amount of activation automatically, but before it is fully recognized, acting to divert attentional activation and full recognition. Or consider electrical responses to unrecognized stimuli. If we assume that these can be triggered by automatic activation, the phenomenon is hardly surprising.

What of priming without awareness, the effect in which a first item reduces reponse times to a second, related item, without being consciously perceived? Again the information-processing account is straightforward. A common explanation of priming, formulated for experiments in which subjects *are* aware of the first item (e.g., Meyer & Schvaneveldt, 1976) proposes that recognition of that item involves activating its conceptual representation in memory. This activation presumably flows to other related conceptual representations, facilitating the recognition of their verbal or pictorial counterparts. In order to extend this account to priming without awareness, we need only assume that activation can proceed from the first representation even when full recognition and conscious identification has not occurred. Just such an assumption is made in other theories. The model of word recognition described in Chapter 2 assumes that early, automatic stages of perceptual processing produce excitatory and inhibitory forms of activation, which flow from one memory representation to related ones. Note that this occurs long before full recognition and awareness.

It is not enough for theories that relate attention to awareness to offer post hoc explanations of findings like priming without awareness or perceptual defense; it is necessary that they make predictions. Theories of pattern recognition and the role of automatic and attentional processes suggest two broad areas for predictions to be made. One concerns the temporal location, within the course of the recognition process, in which one might expect to get automatic versus attentional effects. In order to achieve perception without awareness, it is necessary that peripheral processes can continue to the point where there is automatic access to memory representations, but that nonperipheral processes beyond that point do not achieve full recognition. Disruption of the sensory signal too early, so that it inhibits even initial automatic processes, ought to eliminate the evidence for unaware perception. Disruption of the signal too late ought to bring on full recognition and awareness as well as automaticity.

These temporal patterns have been evidenced in the work by McCauley et al. described previously. The effect of priming one item with a related stimulus is eliminated as the prime's presentation goes well below the threshold duration for identification; awareness of the prime clearly occurs as one goes above the threshold. Marcel (1983a) made a similar point by contrasting two kinds of mask, thought to differ in the location of their effects in the visual system. A post-stimulus mask that contains pattern information (like a jumbled assortment of features of letters) has been theorized to take effect at locations less peripheral than an "energy" mask consisting of random visual "noise" (Turvey, 1973). Consistently with what one would expect, the energy mask not only eliminates conscious perception, but any evidence (in the form of priming effects) for unconscious perception as well. But as we have seen, the pattern mask, with its presumed later point of effectiveness, still allows priming to occur while appearing to curtail awareness.

Marcel (1983a, b) theorizes that a pattern mask interferes with a particular perceptual process, occurring relatively late, called "recovery," which plays a critical role in the conscious experience of perceiving. The recovery process acts on the residual traces or "records" of early processes that describe stimulation at a sensory level; it segments and unitizes the record to produce a conscious product. Recovery manifests attributes of attentional processing other than its lateness of occurrence, including limited capacity and selectivity. It is seen as essential to conscious perception, but by no means to automatic perceptual processing, which is assumed to flow to the highest levels of the memory system regardless of the accessibility of its outputs to recovery and awareness. Thus, although a pattern mask prevents recovery of the records of a masked stimulus, it does *not* prevent other results of the item's processing from having unconscious influences—like priming associated items.

The second broad area in which the attentional view of awareness makes predictions derives from the limited-capacity nature of attentional processing. Along with awareness of a perceived pattern, there should be effects demonstrating capacity demands; when awareness is precluded, capacity limitations should not be evidenced. A finding of McCauley et al. (1980), which can be seen in Figure 3.1, shows one such effect. Note that they measured not only the reduction in naming time to a second stimulus when a related prime stimulus had preceded it (the priming effect), but the actual value of the response time as well. This latter value, the time to name the second of the two pictures, was elevated when the initial picture was presented for the full threshold value, long enough for identification. (Because this elevation was observed regardless of whether the prime was related or unrelated to the second picture, it did not alter the magnitude of the priming effect.) A similar result was found when the effects of identifying the prime were considered. Subjects were told that if able to report a prime picture at the end of a trial, they should, although it was not important. On trials where the prime was presented for a full-threshold duration, it was sometimes reported, sometimes not. When it was reported, naming times for the second picture were longer. In fact, the elevation in response time for the full-threshold condition seemed to derive from just those trials where the prime was reported. This suggests that identifying the prime used attentional capacity that was also needed to identify and name the second picture. Performance seemed actually to be more efficient when subjects were unaware of the prime.

Marcel (1980) demonstrated other evidence for the capacity-limited, selective nature of aware identification, as contrasted with the unlimited nature of automatic, unaware perception. He looked at priming effects of polysemous words, those having more than one meaning. The stimulus items were sequences of three strings of letters, and on some trials, the center string in the triple was masked from aware perception by a closely subsequent pattern. Subjects were to indicate if the first and last stimuli were words. Of particular interest is a triple of words where the center word is polysemous, and the first and third words are related to different meanings of it. Here, for example, is one triple: *tree-palm-wrist*. When no mask was used and subjects were aware of the middle word, the response time to the third word (the time to say it was in fact a word) was as great or greater than the time for three unassociated words, such as *clock-race-wrist*. It seems here that when the first word activated a meaning of the second that was incongruent with the third, there was no facilitating effect of the second. Thus, for example, when *tree* evokes the tree-related meaning of *palm*, *palm* does not facilitate processing of *wrist*.

Such were the results when *palm* was perceived with awareness. In the mask condition, however, the third word in a series like *tree-palm-wrist* was responded to more quickly than in an unrelated series. It appears that *palm* could activate *wrist* even when preceded by *tree*—as long as the subjects were unaware of *palm*. This result is consistent with the idea that perception without awareness is capacity free; *palm* could activate more than one of its meanings on an automatic level even when preceded by *tree*, which biases selection of one meaning. But when *palm* was consciously perceived and preceded by *tree*, limited capacity was devoted to selecting the biased meaning. This precluded *palm* having a facilitating effect on a word related to another of its meanings.

   Given the controversial nature of the priming-without-awareness procedure, it is interesting to find similar evidence of limited-capacity awareness of meaning from a different sort of study. Swinney (1979) investigated the interpretation of polysemous words like *bug*, when they were
heard within a sentence that was either neutral or biased toward a particular meaning. Thus, for example, *bug* could be heard in a sentence
about government buildings that referred to finding *bugs* in a room
(which could mean insects *or* listening devices) or to finding "roaches,
and other bugs" (biased toward the insect meaning). To discern what
meanings were activated, Swinney instructed subjects to understand such
sentences in preparation for a comprehension test. They were also to
watch a screen for strings of letters, and to indicate as quickly as possible
whether the letters formed a word. The basic idea was that responses to
a word on the screen could be speeded, if the word was related to a
meaning that had been activated by the simultaneously heard sentence.
A critical manipulation was that when the sentence biased a particular
meaning for a polysemous word within it (as in biasing *bug* to mean
insect), the visual word on the screen could be related either to that
meaning (like ANT) or to another (like SPY).
   If, when a polysemous word is heard, all of its meanings are aroused,
we might expect it to influence decisions about any related word on the
screen, regardless of the sentence context. Hearing *bug* should facilitate
responding to the printed word *spy*, even when the sentence has previously mentioned insects. In contrast, if only one meaning is active when
a polysemous word is heard in a biased context, then only the printed
word related to the biased meaning (*ant*, but not *spy*, in the insect context)
should be processed faster. Swinney's results indicate that the outcome
depends on how closely together the auditory and printed word occur.
When the visual word is presented at the moment the auditory word
terminates, the relatedness of the two affects response speed, regardless
of any biasing context. Hearing *bug* speeds responses to *spy* even when
the context biases the meaning related to "insect." But if even three
syllables (about 750–1000 msec) intervene between the auditory and visual words, and the sentence biases a particular meaning, only visual
words related to that meaning are processed faster. It seems that by the
time three syllables have passed, selection of one meaning has occurred,
even though several meanings were available earlier.
   Swinney's study supports the idea that many meanings of a word can
be active early in the perceptual process, whereas later one is selected.
Are subjects unaware of the early multiple meanings? Informal data suggest that this is the case. When subjects were asked following the ex-

periment if they had noticed that some words were ambiguous, almost all (81 out of 84) reported they had not. Although this does not preclude that the multiple meanings came into awareness momentarily, at least it seems they were not remembered. It is interesting too that few subjects reported noticing that the visual and auditory words were sometimes related—and then they generally did not report the correct relationships.

In summary, the information-processing view of pattern recognition serves to explain how perception without awareness might occur, and to predict certain aspects of the phenomenon, particularly its temporal location within perceptual processing and its nonselective nature.

I am often asked, in this context, whether perception without awareness can be capitalized on, the most common example being its use in movie theaters to drive the unsuspecting audience toward the refreshment counter. My response is skepticism. First, there are methodological considerations: Can movie screens flash words like "refreshments" at the critical values, such that they are below the duration needed for identification by all observers, yet still sufficient for automatic perceptual processes to be performed? Second, there is the lack of support for behavioral effects of this kind. It is one thing to find that subliminally perceiving a word can delay its identification, or affect the speed with which the meaning of another word is accessed. It is another to find that it can move people out of their seats and into the lobby of the theater. I see no experimental evidence at present for this latter type of effect. For that matter, I have never been in an audience where a number of people first took seats, then made a simultaneous dash for refreshments! Finally, one wonders why subliminal cues are needed in this situation—when overt advertisements can be and often are used. Implicit in subliminal advertising is the theory that subliminal cues are more effective, perhaps because they can't be selectively dismissed. It seems (moral considerations aside) that although theater owners might make the attempt, they should not be too optimistic about the results.

ON-LINE AWARENESS AND THE PERFORMANCE PATHWAY

There are many types of skilled performance. Some, like driving a car, coordinate motoric and perceptual acts; some seem mostly motoric, like walking; still others, like solving geometry problems, are cognitive skills. (Perception could also be considered "performance," but here we restrict the word to processing that produces some observable output as a direct consequence.) As any skill develops, it seems to be characterized by more rapid and efficient performance of the task at hand. But there are also changes in the awareness of performance, and those are the concern of the present section.

Awareness and Performance

As noted earlier, it is commonly claimed that becoming aware of performance serves to impair it. Actually, there are two sub-phenomena that are commonly cited in discussions of awareness and skill. It is said that (1) skilled performers are less aware of what they are doing than unskilled, and (2) that if you force a skilled performer to become aware, his or her performance will decline. Since we cannot observe awareness of performance directly, these claims are in one sense unprovable. However, if we assume that verbalization about the performed act is a reflection of awareness (along the lines of the Ericsson & Simon, 1980, model), we can look for support for these claims in the following way. First, skilled performers will be less able than the unskilled to give a verbal account of what they are doing. Second, efforts to verbally describe some activity concurrently with performance (or possibly even before) will impair a skilled performer, but not an unskilled one.

The first of these claims, that skilled performers are less able to articulate how they perform, is one supported by common personal experience. There are certain activities at which we are all reasonably skilled—reading, recognizing faces or smells, walking. These seem to happen of themselves; it is difficult for us to say *how* we accomplish these performances. In experimental contexts where the development of skill is monitored over some period of time, verbalizations are found to gradually decrease (Anderson, 1982; Chase & Ericsson, 1981; Dean & Martin, 1966; Woodworth, 1938). Chase and Ericsson observed the development of memorization skills in one subject over a period of two years. This subject, a long-distance runner, memorized strings of digits by categorizing groups of them as running times (for example, 0603 became a time for the mile). At first, the budding mnemonist's verbal reports were rich sources for understanding how he performed, but after hundreds of hours of practice, he could articulate little more about his developing skill. Yet his performance continued to improve—from remembering a string of about 40 digits around the 100th session of practice, to 80 digits around the 200th. Ultimately the experimenters reached the point where "verbal reports are of little direct help" (p. 180). Their subject could report *what* he remembered encoding from a string of digits but could no longer report *how*.

The second claim, that concurrent verbalization impairs skilled performance, is also one we can demonstrate for ourselves. Certainly speed and comprehension will suffer if you try to figure out how you understand speech as you are hearing it. For a proper experiment, however, we have to show that it is the concurrent verbalization about the ongoing task that impairs performance, not just the effort of doing two things at once. For example, we might compare the effects of describing speech comprehension while comprehending speech to the effects of describing walking while comprehending speech. The former should be the situation with poorer comprehension.

Unfortunately, studies of this type are difficult to conduct properly, and hard to interpret. Suppose we find that concurrent verbalization about some skilled task interferes with its performance. This could be because the performance had to be slowed down in order to be synchronized with the relatively slow speech about it. I have to play a scale rather slowly on the piano, in order to play each note as I name it—even if I speak quickly. At this point, however, it is not surprising that my scale performance is worse than usual; I am not well practiced at slow scales, but at fast ones. Any other concurrent task that slowed me down equally would probably impair my performance equally. On the other hand, if I don't try to synchronize my performance with my speech about it, and let the music go well ahead of the words, it would not be surprising if the degree of speech-generated interference were no different than if I were speaking about the history of the American Revolution. The content of what I was saying at any moment, whether historical or musical, would be incongruent with what I was doing motorically.

In their review of the concurrent-verbalization literature, Ericsson and Simon (1980) documented a case for the claim that verbalization does *not* impair *unskilled* tasks, although the claim that it *does* impair *skilled* tasks is less clear. The tasks they examined were novel problem-solving situations, with heavy demands on attentional capacity and minimal involvement of perceptual or motor processes that were likely to be highly practiced. In these cases, there was little negative effect of verbalization during performance.

Although there are anecdotal reports on the other aspect of this claim—that highly skilled behaviors are disrupted by verbal description—in the psychological literature (Eccles, 1977; Newell, 1978; Norman, 1982; Polanyi, 1958), experimental evidence is rather sparse, for reasons suggested above. Support for this claim, however, is found in Eccles' (1977) interpretation of some findings of Holmes (1939). Holmes studied patients from World War I who had sustained wounds to one half of their cerebellum, a part of the brain involved in producing smooth movement.

When using limbs that were controlled by the normal half, the patients moved normally. But when using limbs controlled by the wounded half, the patients showed "decomposition of movement," that is jerky, joint-by-joint motions. One of the patients described his situation as follows: "The movements of my left hand are done subconsciously, but I have to think out each movement of my right arm. I come to a dead stop in turning and have to think before I start again." Damage to the cerebellum made it impossible to run off the movement as a whole. To the extent that verbalization which analyzes a skilled movement into components has a similar effect, we might also expect it to be harmful to performance.

Information-Processing Accounts

Can we explain, in information-processing terms, the dropout of awareness as skill develops? Given the premise that awareness is associated with attentional processing, it would appear that the attentional demands of skilled and unskilled performance differ. Theoretical ideas about skill acquisition suggest why this might occur. A critical element in these ideas is that the information-processing structures that control skilled performance are hierarchically organized (see Chapter 2). We must therefore digress to consider further the nature of these hierarchies.

The essence of hierarchical structures, whether perceptual, motoric, or conceptual, is that many elements at one level are nested under a single element at a higher level. The arrangement is not arbitrary, in that elements at the lower level "go together" in some sense to form an integrated unit or chunk. The single element at the higher level can be conceived of as an index or unit for all the components in the chunk. This arrangement has some obvious economical virtues when it comes to performance; control of the single chunking element may suffice to coordinate the individual components.

Hierarchical structures can be used to represent the knowledge used in a motor skill (Arbib, 1981; Keele, 1981; MacKay, 1982; Turvey, Shaw & Mace, 1978) or a cognitive skill (Anderson, 1982; MacKay, 1982; Newell & Rosenbloom, 1981). In the motor areas, for example, a chunk might control a set of limbs and coordinate a gait. In the cognitive area, a chunk might represent a goal that must be met to solve a problem, for example "do a geometric congruence proof by the side-angle-side postulate." The components controlled by this chunk could include several subgoals, such as verifying that two triangles have a side of equal length.

Given hierarchical structures, performance can be likened to an activation of a higher-order control element, which then progresses to sub-

UNSKILLED SYSTEM   **SKILLED SYSTEM**

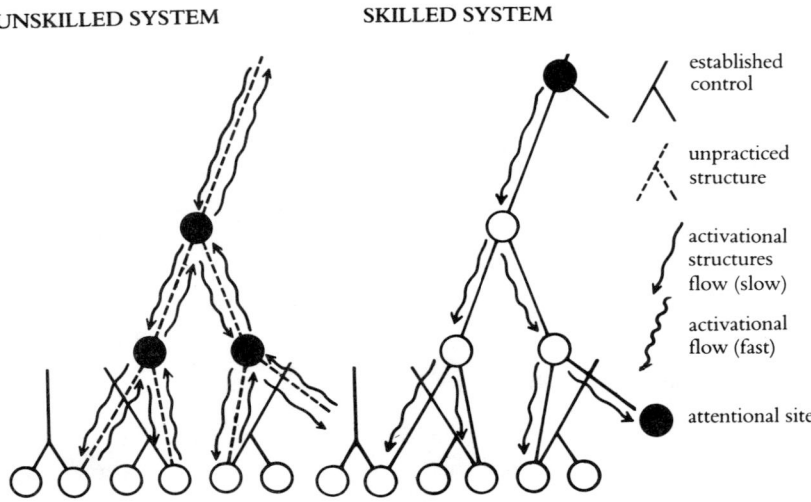

Figure 3.2   Two systems for control of performance, unskilled and skilled.

ordinates, ultimately to effect a response. (For detailed theories of this process, see MacKay, 1982; Rosenbaum, Kenny, & Derr, 1983.) This idea is expressed directly in the motor programming theories described in Chapter 2. A program is a high-level, abstract, control structure that activates more specific muscular substructures, often with minimal need for correction en route. Performance is overtly executed when the activation reaches the bottom of the hierarchy. It is not so different in models of cognitive skills, where a problem is solved when the bottommost goals have been met, and they in turn satisfy higher-order goals, moving in this fashion back up to the top of the hierarchy (Newell & Simon, 1972).

Given the idea that complex performance involves the activation of hierarchically arranged representations, how do these representations change as skill develops, and how do those changes account for concomitant changes in awareness? The answers are complex, but theories of skill development suggest the following, as shown in Figure 3.2. In early stages of motor or cognitive performance, there may be no higher-level control structure for a desired performance; the activity must be implemented by combining existing independent subelements. This requires attentional monitoring of the various subelements and "on-line" correction in accordance with feedback from the performance. But as skill develops, a number of changes occur: New associative pathways are formed, which bring the subelements of performance under a common control element or node. Practiced nodes, including the control element, develop a greater "fluency" (or strength, or propensity for sending activation). The need for feedback from lower elements decreases. Performance speeds up. And most important for present purposes, attentional focus shifts to the control node.

Let us briefly expand on these claims about skill development. They have several sources, including the literature on both cognitive and motor skills. As we shall see, these sources use a somewhat different language, but I would argue that the general ideas agree and persist in a variety of contexts. Here are the claims about how hierarchical structures change with increasing skill:

Formation of New Pathways and Control Structures
If skilled behavior is hierarchically organized, we would expect that building the appropriate hierarchy is part of skill acquisition. Gallistel (1980, p. 367) describes the acquisition of typing skill as: "First, a low level unit of action that has a function in its own right is acquired— striking the "a" key with one's left little finger, for example. Later this unit is brought under the control of higher units, units that sequence the activation of several key-striking motions to produce common words . . ." Similarly, according to Keele (1981, p. 1400), "As a person learns a complex skill, clear shifts in control are seen . . . [W]ith practice the internal control over each movement produces sufficient accuracy that vision is directed not toward each individual component, but rather toward the overall pattern of movement . . ."

A somewhat different idea (Anderson, 1982; Ericsson & Simon, 1980) suggests that the newly formed control system may be structurally different from its predecessors. A basic tenet of Anderson's work, in particular, (and that of others, e.g., Winograd, 1975) is that there are two different kinds of knowledge in memory. "Declarative" knowledge represents articulable facts, whereas "procedural" knowledge represents actions (physical or mental). Declarative knowledge is said to be like an internal sentence; it is also called "propositional" knowledge. In contrast, procedural knowledge is described as a system of "productions," or rules for acting, each consisting of a condition that specifies when to act and an action formulation that specifies how to act. The acquisition of a skill is, in these terms, a gradual conversion of knowledge from the declarative form to the procedural. In the early stages, performance is achieved by using preexisting, more general procedures to operate on or interpret declarative knowledge. The interpretive process is assumed to demand attention. With practice, however, task-specific procedures are developed; these new procedures are direct representations of actions that can be executed without interpretation of the old declarative knowledge.

Consider the case of a beginning tennis player who wants to learn the forehand stroke. He might hold in mind declarative knowledge that indicates where the arm is to be held, how far back it is moved, how swift the forward motion should be, the angle of the racket face, and so on. Given this knowledge, the player applies general procedures for arm movement, which are used for opening doors and shaking hands as well as tennis strokes. After practice, however, all this tedium is bypassed. The player has a procedure that implements the motor movements of the forehand directly and obviates the need to hold in mind the facts of how the forehand should be performed.

Anderson's ideas seem like an expansion of the notion that skills involve the development of new control elements that combine previously separate lower-level representations. The main difference is the idea that the initially applied ad hoc structure uses a different form of knowledge (declarative) than the ultimately developed control node.

With chunk formation comes the possibility that attentional control shifts upward to higher-level chunking nodes (Pew, 1974). This idea seems implicit in the quotations above. It is also compatible with Anderson's theory, which assumes that interpreting declarative knowledge makes heavy demands on attention. Early in learning, low-level declarative knowledge must be stored in working memory (a tennis player may rehearse the forehand while performing it); but with proceduralization, only higher goals, relevant to the procedure as a whole, are stored. Thus there is a shift from attending to facts to attending summary goals.

Changes in "Fluency" of Nodes

The focusing of attention at control nodes may be a specific version of a more general change in the ability of nodes to send and receive activational messages. Consider, for example, a model of speech production proposed by MacKay (1982). This makes use of a hierarchical representation for spoken sentences in a language. The meaning of the sentence as a whole is represented at the uppermost node, subject and predicate nodes branch from that, and further branches descend to words, syllables and so on, terminating in nodes that control the articulation of speech sounds. MacKay proposes that practicing the activation of a node in this hierarchy increases its activation potential, which in turns speeds performance. Further, the effects of practice are greater, the less previous practice the node has had. Suppose that we mentally practice saying the sentence, "Frequent practice is helpful." This will have little effect on the lower nodes representing sounds of speech because we use those all the time, but it will have a large effect on the upper nodes, which represent concepts unique to this particular sentence. Conceptual practice of a sentence in one language should also be effective at speeding up utterance of the same sentence in another language (assuming the speaker is fluent at both), because the nodes representing the sentence's ideas are independent of the particular speech nodes used to express them. MacKay found as predicted that practicing a sentence in one language transfered to a second, while practicing a nonsensical string of words, which had no counterpart conceptual node in the second language, did not.

Elimination of Feedback Use

In most performances there are sources of information that give feedback about success. In the motor system, for example, these include components that send sensory information toward the brain as muscles are used, and information from the eyes about the success of manipulations in space. An action that uses this feedback, following a sequence from act to feedback to adjustment of the act while it is still in progress, is said to be executed "closed loop." A common assumption (e.g., Schmidt, 1975) is that practice converts closed-loop performance to open loop; it reduces or eliminates the use of feedback during performance. The concept of open-loop performance is directly related to the notion of a motor program, as described in Chapter 2. A motor program is a representation of an entire system of performance, which when activated, runs the system with minimal regard to feedback. Thus, to say that practice reduces the need for feedback is similar to saying that practice creates a motor program. Since a motor program is like a chunking node, it should be clear that the idea that practice reduces the use of feedback is also directly related to the chunking idea discussed above.

Speedup of Performance

Performance speeds up with practice. Moreover, the speedup follows a predictable course: The log of the time to perform a behavior is a linear decreasing function of the log of the amount of practice. That is, for each increase in the log of the practice measure, the log of performance time decreases by a constant amount. This holds for tasks as diverse as learning to look for a set of critical letters in a list (Neisser, Novick, & Lazar,

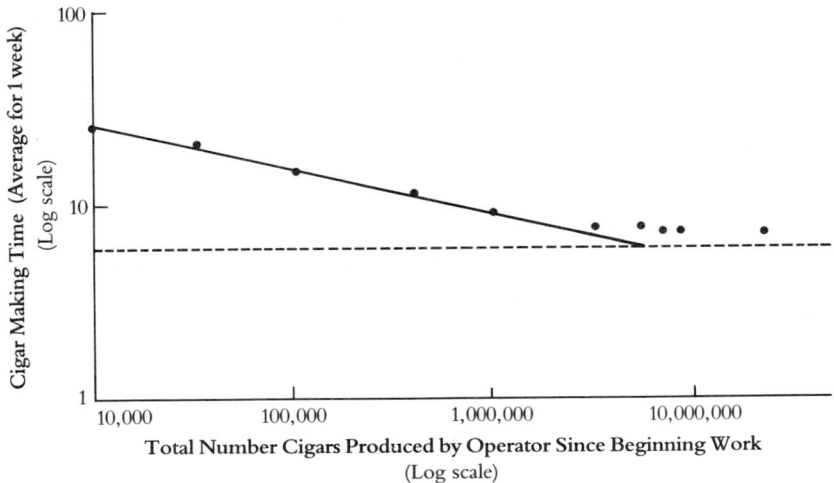

Figure 3.3   Effects of practice on the speed of cigar making with a cigar ma-chine (log scales). Each point represents a different machine operator. The dashed line indicates the minimum performance time imposed by the machine itself. A straight line function has been fit to the first six data points, where operators have room to improve (From Crossman, 1959).

1963) and operating a cigar-making machine (Crossman, 1959). The ef-fect of practice on cigar making speed is shown in Figure 3.3.

Increase in speed of performance with practice is not an independent attribute of skill development; it is related to the other ideas discussed above. When Newell and Rosenbloom (1981) attempted to determine what information-processing changes might lead to the log-log rela-tionship between performance and practice, they found that the rela-tionship is consistent with the idea that practice leads to the formation of new control chunks that integrate several subordinate elements—a fundamental idea. Consider too the relation of feedback to speed. It is commonly assumed that the use of feedback decreases with faster per-formance (e.g., Schmidt, 1975). A source of feedback will be unable to alter an ongoing act, if that act speeds up to the point where it is executed faster than the time required for the feedback to be "fed back" to the point of control. Consider finally the idea that practice increases the ac-tivation potential of nodes. To the extent that performance time depends on the amount or rate of activation accrual, this too implies a speedup with practice. Anderson's (1982) idea of a transition from the use of declarative to procedural knowledge as skill develops also assumes that speedup will occur, since interpreting declarative knowledge will be slower than direct execution of procedures.

Implications for Awareness

To reiterate, information-processing theories of performance seem to converge on the idea that the internal counterparts of skilled performance are hierarchical representations, in which nodes or chunks at one level are superordinate to, and control, nodes or chunks at another level. The development of skill, as it occurs with practice, affects this internal representation in many ways. It has been proposed that practice changes the nature of the hierarchy itself, by instituting new loci of control, and that it changes how those loci operate, improving their speed and efficiency. And for a critically important idea, the locus of attention may move upward as hierarchical control develops.

The idea that attentional control shifts with skill development is especially important because of its implications for awareness of performance. As Pew (1974) has suggested, it seems incorrect to assume that performance becomes entirely automated when a skill is developed. Skilled performance has some of the general characteristics of automatic processing, including rapidity, lack of volitional control of details of execution, and the potential for simultaneous execution with other acts (see, especially, Shaffer, 1981). However, this does not rule out attentional components of skilled acts. The notion of a shift in attention suggests that processes that are subsumed by nodes at lower levels in the hierarchy become automated, while the site at which control is initiated, the attentional focus, moves upward.

Another way to phrase this idea is in terms of performance goals. Attentional monitoring of a performance might be described as evaluating information about its execution, relative to a standard or goal. Changes in the locus of attentional control means that the standard or goal changes, which in turn necessitates a change in the information that is compared to it. A beginning pianist may compare the shape of a finger to a standard, whereas a concert performer evaluates performance against an expressive ideal.

Given this formulation, and the idea that awareness follows attention, we would expect lower levels to drop out of awareness. The higher level at which control initiates should, however, be consciously monitored. Thus a pianist would lose awareness at the muscular level but not become entirely unaware of playing; she would gain awareness of higher levels that control expressive performance. A typist would begin to monitor the word or phrase rather than the finger. A reader would monitor content rather than form; a chess player the field of action rather than individual pieces.

Although these ideas seem intuitively reasonable, some evidence would be useful. It is interesting in this context to reconsider the ideas about awareness and skill discussed earlier. Recall that we began with the common notions that awareness of performance decreases with practice, and that becoming aware impairs execution of a skilled act. These were translated, under the assumption that verbal reports are reasonable indicators of awareness, into the ideas that verbalization about performance decreases with practice, and verbalization about a skill would impair its execution. Yet another formulation of these ideas seems in order, given the present view of skill development and attention. If, as skill develops, attentional focus rises to superordinate levels of a control hierarchy, and if what enters awareness and can be verbalized is directly related to that focus, verbal descriptions of performance should not vanish with practice; they should become more abstract and goal oriented, less concerned with the minute details of execution. Nor should just any kind of verbalization interfere with the performance of a skilled act. Those verbalizations that produce a movement of awareness and attentional focus downward to a previously automated level in the hierarchy should result in impairment.

Concerning the first point, verbalization about performance has been found to change qualitatively with practice (Ericsson and Simon, 1980). Anderson (1982) presented protocols indicating that the verbalizations of students learning to solve geometry problems changed in the way we might expect, from extensive discussion of detailed methods to general goals. (Anderson's theory goes further to suggest why. At early stages, the students' knowledge is declarative, which is capable of articulation. Later, it is procedural and less amenable to verbalization.)

As for the second of these points, given the paucity of experimental work on verbal-generated interference with skilled performance, it is difficult to address. However, it is interesting to consider the data on cerebellum-wounded patients from the present perspective. Recall that the characteristic of their movements, when initiated from the impaired side of the brain, was a decomposition into components. This loss of fluency is just what would be expected to result from lowering the locus of control from the whole-motion level to the individual joints. The anecdotal evidence on this point also suggests that it is analytic verbalization, which breaks down performance into its components, that has a negative effect. Certainly a pianist is not hurt by a general announcement of her intention to play a work by Mozart.

AWARENESS OF PERCEPTION AND PERFORMANCE COMPARED

Superficially, the two information-processing pathways just discussed may seem quite different. One concerns the input side of information-processing, the other output. One—awareness in perception—is assessed with phenomenal reports of the product, knowledge of *what* one is perceiving. The other—performance—is assessed with phenomenal reports of the process, knowledge of *how* one is performing; the "what" of performance is observed directly.

Yet these two phenomena are unified by certain common assumptions. Most important is the idea that awareness is associated with attentional, rather than automatic, processing. Another is the idea that automaticity is a characteristic of skill. Both perception and output performance can be skilled and relatively unaware, or unskilled and performed with greater awareness.

The development of perceptual skill may be less obvious than the development of performance skills. Yet, most of us remember something of our transition from lip-moving reading to fluent processing of written language. The acquisition of perceptual skills in other areas is a principal component of what we call expertise: reading X-rays, sexing chickens or distinguishing stitches in knitting.

One aspect of the previous discussion that seems to differentiate the perceptual and performance pathways is the emphasis on hierarchical structure and control in the case of performance, but not perception. However, this difference is not as great as it appears. As Chapter 2 makes clear, theories of perception also make use of the concept of hierarchical representations, in which activation of nodes culminates in perceptual identification.

It is interesting to question whether awareness of perception, as skill develops, is associated with higher-level nodes in these hierarchies. This would move the perceptual pathway closer to performance. Examples from everyday life suggest that awareness of perceptual processing does accrue to superordinate levels of representation. We read and hear words or even phrases, for example, rather than component letters or phonemic sounds. We see chairs, not legs and seats.

Turning to experimental evidence, several lines of research support the suggestion that our conscious perceptual identification responses, within skilled domains, correspond to relatively abstract or high-level representations. By skilled domains I mean perception of objects and language, areas in which most people have extensive practice. It should be noted that the research of interest does not indicate that on-line awareness in perception occurs at the "highest possible" level of representation. Indeed, it is not clear what that level should be. In the case of an object (like a chair), the "highest possible" level, if defined by the most abstract category into which the object is classified, would be something like "nonliving thing." We would not expect chairs to be perceptually identified at such a level. In the case of hearing or reading language, where the hierarchical levels might be defined by how much of the input they encompass (e.g., features vs. letter vs. words), the "highest possible" level might be the most inclusive, in which case we might expect conscious apprehension of a novel to occur only after its reading was completed! Clearly, the highest-possible hypothesis is not well formulated and just plain wrong. Marcel (1983b) has suggested that perceptual recognition occurs at the "most functionally useful" level, which becomes higher as we learn about perceived stimuli. In any case, it seems reasonable to state that conscious perceptual recognition of objects and linguistic inputs occurs at a level more abstract or inclusive than the postulated bottom of hierarchy, whatever that may be.

Rosch and associates (e.g., Rosch, Mervis, Gray, Johnson, and Boyes-Braem, 1976) examined a possible hierarchy for the representation of common objects, and in so doing, provided some evidence relevant to the present hypothesis. They divided the categorical representation of a variety of objects into a three-level hierarchy, where the levels were called subordinate, basic, and superordinate. The basic level was defined by several criteria, including the fact that it was the level at which the object was generally named. Thus, "chair" is a basic-level category, "kitchen chair" is subordinate, and "furniture" is superordinate in this hierarchy.

Basic-level categories have important characteristics which make them good candidates for the culmination of perceptual recognition: Members of the *same* basic category have a lot in common, *and* members of two *different* basic categories have relatively little. In contrast, members of the same superordinate category may have little in common (like chairs and lamps), and members of two different subordinate categories may be very similar (like kitchen chairs and dining room chairs). In short, dividing the world of objects at the basic level is efficient, in that it maximizes our ability to categorize and discriminate. Several studies of Rosch et al., converge on the idea that perceptual recognition occurs at the basic level, rather than the subordinate (or superordinate). One found that subjects are faster at identifying a picture of an object when told to look for a basic-level name, like a chair, than when told to look for a subordinate (kitchen chair) or superordinate (an article of furniture). This occurs even though "kitchen chair" specifies more features of the to-be-recognized object. Here is one case that supports the notion of high-level awareness in pattern recognition.

This same notion has been made explicit by LaBerge (1981, p. 68) in reference to pattern recognition in reading. According to LaBerge, "At some point the features and the relations spanning the entire pattern are 'fused' or reintegrated into a single unit. Attention that was formerly directed successively to component features and to relations between features now is directed to one entity. This is the *unitization* stage. Attention is probably still required for maintenance of this new unitization, but the nature of its focus has changed from one perceptual level to a higher level." In support of this idea, LaBerge musters a variety of findings. For one (Terry, Samuels, & LaBerge, 1976), when subjects were asked to categorize a single word (e.g., to classify "bear" as animal or nonanimal), the time to respond was independent of the number of letters in the word. Since we know that a hallmark of attentional processing is that more applications (here, more letters to process) require more time, this result indicates that attention is not being used to process the individual letters in the word. The word level appears to be the unit where attention is applied.

In contrast, when words were presented in mirror-image form, word length had a pronounced effect on response time for the same task. This implicates skill in the phenomenon of unitization. When letters in words are mirror reversed, previous skills no longer apply, and now attention is devoted to the individual letters (or, at least, units below the word level). As a further indication of the role of practice and skill development, Samuels, LaBerge, and Bremer (1978) examined the effects of word length on categorization time for different grade levels. Second-graders showed a pronounced word-length effect, indicative of letter-by-letter processing. This effect decreased with higher grade levels up to college students, who again showed no word-length effect.

Another task suggesting word-unit recognition in reading has been used extensively by Healy (reviewed briefly in Healy, 1981). This task is particularly interesting because it tests subjects' awareness of letters in a direct way. The subjects are asked to read a passage of text and circle every instance of some target letter, such as t. In other words, they are asked to circle letters of which they are aware. One important finding is that they make more errors in very common words in which the target letter occurs than in rare words (*the* is missed often, *thy*, infrequently). Healy suggests this occurs because common words like *the* are processed and identified as high-level units. Their individual letters are not necessarily processed to the point of aware identification, because processing of low-level units may be terminated once identification at a higher level has occurred.

In the study of speech perception it has long been acknowledged that recognition processes operate on segments far more inclusive than the individual primitive components of spoken language. It has been shown, in a way not dissimilar to the findings of Healy in reading, that portions of speech can be eliminated and replaced with a nonspeech sound without the listener's realizing it (e.g., Samuel, 1981; Warren, 1970). This would not occur if the hearer were aware of each phoneme in the signal.

Practiced recognition of patterns of various types appears to produce a conscious output at a level of representation that is accessed relatively late in perception, and "high" in a hierarchical sense, however, we define the hierarchy. This brings awareness in the perceptual pathway closer to awareness on the output side, given the argument that attentional control is focused at high hierarchical levels in skilled performance.

At the beginning of this chapter, I suggested that we might enhance our understanding of both awareness and information processing by assuming an association between awareness and attention and exploring its implications. This general assumption appears to have been useful. It suggested certain properties of awareness, such as occurrence late in the stream of processing, variation with practice, and limited capacity, which have received experimental support. In addition, it can be usefully applied to certain common beliefs about awareness or the lack thereof, suggesting when and why they might be true, and removing them from the realm of mystical phenomena. These can be considered some of the benefits of applying the information-processing approach to the study of awareness. Conversely, considering the nature of awareness and common beliefs about it has led to an appreciation of commonalities between perception and performance, potentially benefitting students of information processing as well.

4

Awareness and Memory Retrieval: The Retrieval Process

There are many things that I know and can remember right now to my own satisfaction. There are many I think I know but can't report right now, many about which I am uncertain, many that I don't know and know I don't know, many that I think I don't know but will realize later than I do. There are things I know about what I know—how well I know it, or where I came to know it. Whew!

Here are some of the things I know: days of the week, what I ate for dinner last Saturday, where I learned that John Kennedy had been assassinated. Here are some things I think I remember correctly, but am not sure: formulas for differentiating terms of the form ax^n, who told me that babies were made by sitting on a blanket. Here are some things I think I know, although I can't prove it right now: the days of the week in French, what I ate for dinner last Christmas day. And some things I'm sure I don't know: days of the week in Polish, how to rhumba . . .

How do I evaluate what I know? In a variety of ways. I may try to remember, and if I can, figure that I know. I may try to check my memory against some factual record, or I may just assess how confident I feel about what I am remembering. Perhaps I remember where I learned something that I am remembering, and perhaps I don't and am afraid that I imagined it. Why do I think I know even when I can't remember? I may feel that the present circumstances aren't adequate to produce a report, but that others would be. I can't describe my father's face, but I am sure I could pick out his photograph. I could learn the days of the week in French more rapidly than if I had never learned them; this shows I have some residual memory. I'm pretty sure of many things I don't know because I know I never had the opportunity to learn them. (In the case of the rhumba, it's more the agility than the opportunity.) Other things I think I don't know because I keep trying to remember them and can't.

All of these questions and attempted answers concern what I am calling "epistemic" awareness, that is, awareness of the contents of memory. (Recall that epistemology is the philosophical branch concerned with the theory of knowledge and knowing.) Awareness of this sort is acquired through a complex process called *retrieval* from memory, which incorporates (see Chapter 2) several component subprocesses.

The concern of this chapter and the next is the relationship between awareness and retrieval. We can divide this question into two parts. First, we can ask how aware one is of the events that occur during the actual act of retrieving, between some cue to remember and the final outcome, whether it is success or failure. This is a question about on-line awareness; awareness of cognitive operations more than perception or performance. Second, we can concern ourselves with epistemic awareness, which I assume is provided by the act of retrieving. In other words, retrieval is a complex process aimed at revealing the contents of our memory. We can differentiate between awareness of those contents—what is re-trie*ved*—and awareness of how we got them—what is retrie*ving*. The latter topic will be discussed here; the former, in the chapter that follows.

COMPONENTS OF RETRIEVAL

The retrieval process as a whole is generally initiated with some cue or memory "probe," perhaps environmental like a smell or someone's speech, perhaps internally generated, like signals of hunger that cause one to retrieve the fact of missing breakfast. The cue that is present at the start of retrieval may be modified by the rememberer and used to generate further cues; for this reason *cue generation* is considered one of the subprocesses of retrieval. If I am given a cue "Recall your high school classmates," I may think of the high school building or the style of clothing of that era, which provides me with further cues. The process that makes contact with stored information is often called *search*. Some information that is turned up by the search process may be the current target of retrieval; it may be in the to-be-remembered set. But other information may be accessed that is not the current target. For example, asked to remember high school classmates, I may recall the names of some teachers. For this reason another retrieval subprocess is required: the *decision* process indicates whether accessed information is actually called for in the current context of retrieval. Finally, the act of retrieval usually culminates in some sort of statement about what is being remembered. This requires a process of *response generation*. I clearly remember the class "jock," but the process of generating his name is failing right now. Thus, I have fulfilled most of retrieval, but can't really say I am remembering.

As an illustration of the entire retrieval process, consider what happens when I ask you to retrieve "16th President of the United States." You may be able to retrieve this directly, from my probe, or you may generate some cues of your own—16th President sounds familiar, must be famous, might have occurred 90 years or so after the Union was formed, given the usual Presidential term of 4 to 8 years. You might do an ordered search through the set of Presidents or a less directed search, just generating Presidents in the hope that you will realize one was the 16th. For each candidate President, you have to make a decision as to whether it is the desired response. Washington certainly isn't; Grant might be. Finally you decide, "16th President, that's the Civil War guy, what was his name?", ultimately generating the called-for response, "Abraham Lincoln."

Although theorists often speak of the processes of cue generation, search, decision, and response generation as if they were discrete and clearly identifiable, in fact they are closely interrelated. Cue generation is actually like an encoding process, in that an external cue is perceived and related to other information in memory. Search is inseparable from cue generation to some extent, because the act of searching memory may provide access to some information that is related to the to-be-remembered items, which acts in turn as a cue for further search. As we shall also see, some cues are very complete and provide direct access to the desired information in memory. In this case, encoding the cue and searching are virtually synonymous. Response generation may be like a retrieval process in its own right, in which the to-be-remembered information a phonemic or articulable representation of items that have been accessed and are available for report.

It is also important to note that these subprocesses of retrieval do not necessarily proceed in a strict temporal order. Retrieval may cycle back and forth among subprocesses or even execute some simultaneously. Decision may be attempted while search is ongoing and become successful after a sufficient amount of information has been accessed.

How important each of the components of retrieval is varies with the retrieval situation, which in memory research often takes the form of a explicit memory test. If I ask you whether a picture of Abraham Lincol is a familiar or unfamiliar person, I am minimizing cue generation (by giving you the picture as a cue) and search (by providing a direct cue to the to-be-remembered information). I am also facilitating response generation by telling you what responses are possible (familiar/unfamiliar). If I ask you to name the picture, response-generation difficulty goes up. On the other hand, your decision process would be more difficult if I gave you a picture of someone you had once seen incidentally, as happens when witnesses to a crime must pick out suspects from a set of mug shots.

AUTOMATIC AND ATTENTIONAL COMPONENTS OF RETRIEVAL

Being aware of retrieving while it occurs is much like being aware of other processes as they progress on-line. Following the arguments of Chapter 3, we might expect to be aware of what is going on during retrieval to the extent that attention is required. If certain aspects of the retrieval process occur automatically, we should not be aware of them; if they are effortful and attention-demanding, we should. As we shall see, matters are not this transparent. I will begin the discussion by examining whether there are automatic and attention-demanding components of the complex retrieval process, and then consider how aware we might be of the automatic and attention-demanding components.

Direct and Associative Search in Retrieval

Laboratory experiments in which subjects learn lists of items are a rich source of information relevant to automatic and attentional components of retrieval. Typically these studies present an arbitrary set of items (perhaps twenty) like the words "furniture" and "brickbat." Later memory is tested for these items in one of two ways. In a *recall* test, subjects are typically asked to recall everything from the list they studied. In a typical *recognition* test, subjects are presented with previously studied, to-be-remembered items, and "distractor" items now being given for the first time in the experimental context; their task is to say which items are which. Thus the two tests differ considerably in the nature of the cues they provide. A recall test is characterized by minimal provision of overt cues or probes, like "list of words." A recognition test is characterized by provision of more robust cues, usually in the form of the to-be-remembered information ("furniture?" "brickbat?") itself.[1]

The essential difference between the recall and recognition testing procedures lies in the experimenter-provided cues. We would naturally expect this to produce differences in the subject's cue-generation component of retrieval. There is more need to generate cues in recall than recognition. What is less obvious is that the two testing procedures also differ in their demands on the search component of retrieval.

Recalling a set of items is often described as involving an *associative* search in memory; access to one item's representation leads along pathways or associations to provide access to another. In recalling U.S. Presidents, recall of Lincoln may lead to recall of Grant, through their common association to the Civil War. These chaining notions of the search process are supported by the common finding from list-learning studies that attempts to mentally tie items together at the time of encoding (thinking of "furniture" in relation to "brickbat," for example—e.g., Tulving, 1962) ultimately help recall. Presumably, associative encoding of this sort promotes the formation of chains, connecting items in the list to one another and to representations of the list context. These chains are then useful in the associative search at the time of retrieval.

Whether recognition similarly requires an associative search of memory has been a matter of debate (see Klatzky, 1980, for review). It might seem that the recognition "cue," which is said to be a "copy" of the to-be-remembered item itself, would be such a direct and effective means of gaining access to memory that no associative search would be necessary. However, that's not necessarily true. No cue in a recognition test can ever be an exact copy, because the information stored in memory is an encoded version of what was presented, which may include particular interpretations of the presented material and other components of the event. If I am given the word *field* as part of a set of words to remember, I may encode the meaning *baseball field*, in association with *list of words, experiment, green room*, and so on. Later presentation of *field* is not a copy of this complex encoding of an entire event.

This point has been made in some clever experiments (e.g. Tulving & Thomson, 1973), which make clear that recognition testing does not inevitably eliminate the need for an associative search process. A search is likely, for example, if an item is initially presented in a way that biases the encoding of one meaning (*cold* is presented with *ground*) and tested in a way that does not provide direct access to the meaning (*cold* is tested in the context of *hot*, or worse yet, *sneeze*). In this case, the so-called copy cue is far from a copy of the originally encoded version of the item, and a search for the encoded version may become necessary. Recognition cues generally reduce but do not necessarily eliminate the demands on the search process.

The search along associative pathways that occurs in a recall or recognition test of memory culminates in access to some representation of knowledge. In this sense, the search process is similar to another that accesses representations in memory—pattern recognition. There are, however, some obvious differences between the two kinds of access. One difference is in speed: the perceptual recognition of a word, as in reading, is very fast; the access to a word's representation given a cue like *words on first list* is much slower. The difference in speed may reflect differences in practice: perceptual recognition of words occurs frequently, and makes use of habitual pathways in long-term memory, whereas following associations among the representations of various words (especially when they were not associated until they were arbitrarily aggregated by an experimenter) is quite unpracticed. Another difference is in the pathways that are followed in the search process: a critical progression of memory access in pattern recognition is "bottom up", from representations of knowledge that are closely tied to the sensory system, to more abstract, conceptual knowledge units. In contrast, for search as it occurs in recall, the sensory level is relatively unimportant. Associative search in recall is generally depicted as progressing among representations for *concepts*, like those for "list," "brickbat," and "furniture."

In considering different types of access to memory representations, it is particularly interesting to consider recognition-testing situations. As I have indicated, recognition testing—like recall—may require an associative search among conceptual representations of list items in memory. On the other hand, if a recognition test provides a "copy" cue for a list item, that cue is read, and the pattern-recognition process provides access to its meaning in a direct, perceptual manner.

Certain theories of the recognition process (Atkinson & Juola, 1973; Mandler, 1980) have used such distinctions among means of accessing memory, in order to account for variations in performance. These theories assume that when a previously presented, now to be recognized, item appears on a test, its memory representation may be accessed by two types of processes. One is quite direct and occurs very quickly after the copy cue is presented, like the activation of a memory location that occurs in pattern recognition. The other is an indirect associative search similar to that described in remembering United States Presidents; it is initiated somewhat later and is more time consuming. Baddeley (1982), in making a similar distinction, has called this sort of effortful process "recollection."

Figure 4.1 illustrates the two kinds of access schematically. We see that before presentation of a word like *cat* on a list, the word itself has a

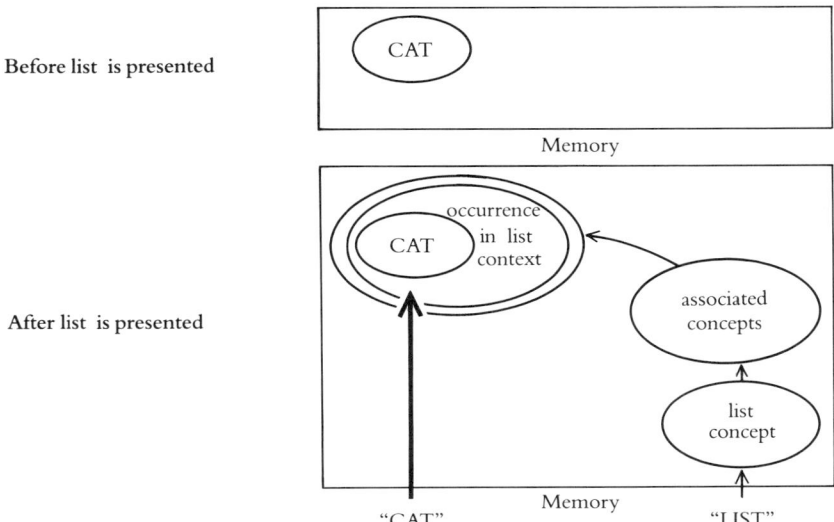

Figure 4.1   Two means of accessing the representation of a word (cat) presented as part of a list: directly, when cued with the word itself, or indirectly, when cued with the list context.

representation in memory. Its presentation incorporates into memory a representation of the "episode" in which cat occurred on a list (denoted by a double line), which is in turn associated with other memory representations. Retrieval of the cat-on-list episode can occur through two avenues. Cueing with *cat* leads directly to the episodic representation, whereas cueing with *list* leads to it indirectly, through various other associations.

Going a step further, we can relate these two kinds of memory access to the experiments of Schneider and Shiffrin (1977—see Chapter 2), where subjects were tested on recognizing items from a very short list of targets, and speed was as important as accuracy. When the subjects were well practiced on items that were consistently used as targets, they responded quite rapidly, and they manifested direct access and a lack of item-by-item list search by responding as rapidly when their list included several targets as when it had only one. In contrast, lack of such training produced evidence for a search through the individual items in the list of targets, in the form of more errors, longer response times, and a direct relationship between response time and the number of targets in the current list.

We see that in these latter experiments, two search processes appear to be possible, just as in the more conventional recognition test of memory. It seems like a short step to draw a connection between the automatic and attentional processes assumed to underlie the two patterns of performance in the Shiffrin/Schneider task, and the two search processes described above, for recognition of longer, unpracticed lists. Schneider and Shiffrin proposed that the faster, more accurate search for practiced targets was automatic, whereas the other search was attentional. Similarly, we can speculate that the direct, speedy search process proposed in theories of recognition for longer lists may be largely automatic, or at least relatively undemanding of attention, whereas the indirect associative search along pathways that relate items in memory demands attention. This would be consistent with the idea that the first, faster search process is much like pattern recognition, with its automaticity. One would not expect an associative search among representations of words on an arbitrary list to be automatic because the very arbitrariness of the list's composition means that those associations are not practiced. (Of course, associative chaining among highly related words *can* be automatic, as was indicated in the discussion of unconscious priming in Chapter 3.)

The suggestion that memory retrieval can occur either through automatic or attentional processes is like a mirror image of the previously described (Chapter 2) proposal of Hasher and Zacks (1979), in regard to encoding. They suggested that some information from the environment is encoded into memory directly, without intention and attention, whereas encoding of other types of information requires attentional processing. Most important for present purposes, the formation of associations among arbitrary items in a list is a good example of an attentional encoding device, which aids memory for the items but demands capacity. It seems consistent, then, to propose that following those arbitrary associations at the time of retrieval would also be an attention-demanding process. Further support for this idea is found in one of Hasher and Zacks's criteria for attentional encoding—namely, that it should vary as a function of capacity differences in individuals, as might be influenced by age. Aging appears to affect performance with recall testing—where the demands for associative search are relatively great—more than recognition—where associative search is minimized, due to the provision of strong cues (Craik, 1977). This is at least consistent with the idea that associative search in list-learning tasks demands attention.

Finally, Craik (1983) has reported some fairly direct evidence that the retrieval of words in an arbitrary list demands attention: it is interfered with by a simultaneous attention-demanding task. The relevant result is that fewer words were recalled in a limited time when subjects simultaneously sorted playing cards than when they did not. Interestingly, card-sorting did not impair recognition of words, where search demands presumably were minimal.

In summary, the search component of the retrieval process seems to take various forms. In particular, we can distinguish between two means of accessing some targeted, to-be-remembered, representation in memory. One is "direct" search, which accesses the representation along practiced perceptual pathways; the other, "associative" search, which makes use of less habitual pathways among concepts that are related to the to-be-remembered information. These search mechanisms are likely to be implemented under different circumstances. To the extent that direct search is like the bottom-up component of pattern recognition, which links external stimuli with memory representations, it necessitates that the retrieval cue be a "good" stimulus. This means that the retrieval cue for direct search should bear a close resemblance to the to-be-remembered item. This is the case in most recognition testing, but not recall. Recall, more than recognition, should demand the associative type of search.

The two search mechanisms are also assumed to differ in their demands on attentional capacity, although the direct/associative search distinction does not correspond to a neat automatic/attentional dichotomy. It seems more appropriate to describe search processes in terms of an attentional continuum: as a search relies more on nonhabitual, novel associations in the memory structure, it demands more attention. Direct search, as it has been described, is achieved by activation of well established memory pathways and lies at the low end of the continuum. Associative search uses attention in varying amounts. As it occurs during recall of an arbitrary list, the search process appears to demand a great deal of attention; during recall of more practiced lists (the alphabet, U.S. Presidents) it might demand less.

Decisions Following Direct and Associative Search

Recognition and recall tests require that rememberers make overt, conscious decisions about what they remember. Whether access to potential to-be-remembered information is direct or associative, automatic or attentional, it must provide some basis for these decisions, in order to effect a successful report. We would, however, expect the basis for decision to be somewhat different, depending on the type of search. Direct search is assumed to provide access to a to-be-remembered item alone (except for other knowledge activated automatically during perception), whereas associative search turns up the item as part of a larger body of information. Thus, recognition decisions that follow automatic search should rely more on information about the item per se, whereas recall decisions and those recognition decisions that follow associative search should also use information about the larger context in which the item was retrieved.

In agreement with this reasoning, Mandler (1980) has suggested that recognition performance can have either an intraitem or interitem basis. The first is a property of an item itself, and the second a property of items in relation to other information. According to his model, either of these can underlie decisions in recognition, and they act independently. More specifically, it is assumed that a recognition test first provides a *familiarity* value for the cued item itself, which may produce a recognition decision. If familiarity is insufficient, the item may be recognized on the basis of a slower process that retrieves associations to other items along with the item itself, including associations that define it as a member of the to-be-remembered set. Retrieval of an association to "U.S. President" may lead to the decision that Taft was one. Retrieval of associations to other list items or to the experimental context may lead to the decision that "cold" was on a list.

Work by Jacoby and Dallas (1981) provides further support for the notion that there are two bases for decision in memory recognition. They presented words in a list, then examined the influence of a variety of experimental manipulations—they did this not only for the usual recognition memory task, but also for the task of identifying the words when they were briefly presented and followed by a pattern mask. The recognition task provides a measure of how well the list is remembered (the percent of items that are recognized); the perceptual-identification task provides a measure of how readily its words are perceived (the percent of words identified).

These experiments showed that a number of variables that would be expected to influence the formation of associative pathways (relating list words to other concepts) affected recognition memory performance without changing the rate of perceptual identification. One such variable was how meaningfully a word was interpreted during a list presentation, which was manipulated by the nature of the instructions given to the subject. Other variables, like the number of times a word in the list was presented, influenced both recognition and the perceptual-identification task. Words that were presented more often were both recognized more and perceived better.

Based on these results, there seem to be two families of variables that influence performance on a memory-recognition test. Some variables influence the ease of perceiving as well as memory recognition. Others influence only recognition, not perception. These latter tend to be (though not exclusively) variables that manipulate associative encoding, that is, the degree to which list items are related with each other and with other concepts during the study interval. These results therefore support the notion that recognition decisions have two bases, one of which is related to perceptual activity, the other relying on conceptual associative connections. From preceding discussions, we might suggest further that these two types of decision follow different means of searching memory. The perceptually based decision follows direct access to memory representations, along pathways used in perceptual recognition, whereas the associatively based decision follows indirect access along memory pathways and utilizes the interitem knowledge that such a search provides.

AWARENESS AND ASSOCIATIVE SEARCH

If a search process is effortful and attention demanding, we should be aware of it (assuming awareness is related to attention). I have characterized the attentional search process as indirect, following (nonhabitual) pathways between the memory representations of to-be-remembered information and associated ideas or context. In asking how aware we are of this search process, it is necessary to consider what there is to be aware *of.* A theoretical distinction that is relevant is one between "products" and "processes" of mental activity. Proponents of this distinction suggest that we might be aware of the *products* of associative search.

What might these products be? In general, the product/process distinction differentiates between mental representations of information (products) and the mental activities (processes) that operate on them. Nisbett and Ross (1980) have defined a mental process as the means by which one internal event influences another; it is to be distinguished from the contents of the mind. Mandler (1975, p. 231) has described a process as a transformation on internal objects, events, and relations, which are the products of mind. In the context of associative search, products might be linked-together conceptual representations. Processes would include the activities that search out the interconnections.

The distinction between products and processes has been a source of controversy among psychologists; its relation to awareness, even more so. The theorists cited above have proposed that processes, unlike products, cannot be consciously observed—they can only be inferred on the basis of products. Ericsson and Simon (1980) have countered that anything that can come under focal attention can be verbalized (and thus must be conscious)—and that this includes processes, as long as they are not automated. To round out this set of opinions, White (1980) has argued that the process/product distinction has not been formulated well enough to render testable any claims about its relationship to consciousness!

In the more limited domain of memory retrieval, however, it may be possible to make an attempt at distinguishing between products and processes and to relate that distinction to awareness of associative search. Consider this complex case of retrieval. Suppose I try to remember what I did on Thanksgiving Day in 1980. I conceive of my efforts as something like the following: "Let me see, in 1980 I spent the year in Santa Barbara, and I don't think we went away for Thanksgiving, because we usually take a brief trip at Christmas. That wasn't the year we met my friend Fantasia in Los Angeles, was it? No, that meeting must have been earlier, because she wasn't married at the time, and she's been married for at least five years. So in 1980 I was almost certainly at home, in which case we had a bunch of people over, because that's what we generally do." I have deliberately chosen this example because, by setting myself a difficult memory problem, I become aware of many things during the retrieval interval. Intervening information, in the form of other retrieved facts and inferences that I encountered on the way to my final solution, entered awareness—as evidenced by my ability to report them. These intervening retrieved data are a product—at least, a byproduct—of retrieval. On this basis, then, I can say I was aware of products of the retrieval effort. But what about processes? This question is more difficult because there is no clear definition of a process. If we define the retrieval process as whatever occurred during the interval between contemplating 1980 and my decision that we had guests for dinner, I was aware of it (at least in part). But if we define the "process" here as the mechanism by which I made the transition from one product or retrieved fact to another, I cannot say that I was aware of it.

More systematic research on this question supports the view that we are aware of intermediate products of memory search (in the sense I described above), and shed further light on the question of awareness of processes. Read and Bruce (1982) looked at extended retrieval efforts following "memory blocks," states where people felt they knew something but couldn't retrieve it easily. These states were elicited by presenting subjects with cues—photographs or verbal descriptions—to the names of somewhat obscure entertainers and asking for their names. (The verbal descriptions included such data as shows the entertainer had performed in.) Once memory blocks occurred, they were tracked over a period of up to three weeks or so.

Subjects were asked to describe what they were aware of during their search of memory, once their memory block had been overcome and they had successfully retrieved the name. These descriptions seemed to be classifiable into various nonmiscellaneous categories, some concerned with what was retrieved, others concerned with how it was retrieved. Subjects were aware of retrieving partial information about the structure of the name, such as its length or initial letter; they consciously retrieved contextual information, such as a name of the person's spouse, or events in the career; and they retrieved associated visual or auditory information, such as facial appearance when the cue was verbal. There was also awareness of certain strategies for retrieval. One was feature focusing—consciously directing attention to some information about the person, such as a particular scene from a film or the sound of a voice. Another was trying to generate a series of names that were semantically or structurally related to the potential target name.

Read and Bruce propose that the kinds of things subjects reported in their task are primarily "products," that is, they are content related to the to-be-remembered name, rather than the internal processes that resulted in those contents. Even when the reports were concerned with strategies such as generating names or focusing on a feature, the comments revealed more about the contents produced by the strategy than the strategy itself. Even if subjects were aware of strategies, it can be argued that strategy is distinct from process. A strategy is more like a plan for what processes should be implemented.

Williams (1978) and Santos-Williams (Williams & Santos-Williams, 1980) had earlier reported similar data on extended retrieval efforts. They asked subjects to think aloud while trying to remember the names of all their high school classmates. This continued for up to 10 one-hour sessions, one per day. (So effortful did the subjects find these sessions that they could not be coaxed into more than an hour at a time.) In addition to cataloguing the phenomena of retrieval, these researchers analyzed what the subjects said during the retrieval effort (note that the Read/Bruce reports came after completion of retrieval). The basic facts, or propositions, that subjects uttered were divided into five categories, two of which are of particular interest in this context. "Strategy" comments are one category: "I'm trying to think of the people that sat around me (in English class)," or "I'm trying to think of the sports we played and who's on which team" (Williams & Santos-Williams, 1980, p. 675). As suggested above about strategies in general, strategy comments do not describe processes, so much as plans for how to implement them. "Processing" comments are the second category. Rather than describe a process per se, these summarize a previous sequence of retrieval attempts and/or signal changes in processing, such as, "I can't remember anyone else in that class."

In short, comments elicited on-line during retrieval and after show evidence that the intermediate points in an effortful memory search—contents, plans for implementing the search, decision points, and summaries—are consciously experienced. Thus it would be a mistake to say that there is no awareness of the retrieval process, as a whole. On the other hand, there is little report of making transitions between individual pieces of retrieved data. As we saw earlier, it would seem that some processes enter awareness, some do not, depending one what we choose to call a process.

It is not possible to resolve the controversy over whether processes, like products, come under awareness, without refining our definitions of process. Processes are descriptions at potentially many levels. At one extreme, we would not expect awareness of such microprocesses as neural transmission. At another level are macroprocesses like "thinking," about which no summary statement of awareness can be made. A strategy like planning to run through the list of Presidents from Washington forward might be considered as a process between these two levels; search may be closer to the microprocess level. Given the variety of processes and levels at which they may be described, it seems inappropriate to make *one* statement about awareness of processing that is to be true without qualification. (White, 1980, has made a similar argument.)

If, on the other hand, we restrict ourselves to the context of memory retrieval, and make clear what we call a process, more can be said about awareness of products and processes. Introspective verbal reports about rather complex retrieval problems, which appear to be effortful, time-consuming, and attention-demanding, suggest that retrievers are aware of information of certain types. These include what I have called "products"—information related to the target of retrieval that is accessed during the effort to retrieve. Also included are strategies that guide the retrieval effort. Considered as a whole the retrieval "process" does proceed with awareness. At a more microsopic level, processes like making associative transitions are not generally reported as coming into awareness.

AWARENESS AND DIRECT SEARCH

If we are aware of retrieving concepts that are related to a to-be-remembered target and strategies for organizing the search process, what is there to be aware of about direct search? I have characterized direct search as proceeding to to-be-remembered information without accessing associated conceptual information of the sort that seems to provide intermediate conscious products in attentional search. Direct search might be called a "pure process." Its only conceptual "product" is its endpoint, the searched-for information.

And if direct search is an automatic process, we shouldn't be aware of the search process itself. I do not mean to say that we should be entirely unaware of retrieving. Once information in memory has been accessed, albeit automatically and directly, we may become aware of its activation (we know we are reading or hearing a word) and have conscious feelings of familiarity. These are the end products. I am suggesting, however, that we make a distinction between direct access to memory, which may progress without on-line awareness, and conscious feelings (like the degree of familiarity) that follow that access.

REMEMBERING WITHOUT AWARENESS

The distinction between accessing the residue of past experiences in memory, and conscious feelings about what is remembered, is particularly important in considering the phenomenon of "remembering without awareness." In discussing perceptual recognition, I proposed (with considerable hindsight) that if an experimental manipulation were to cut off the conscious recognition response that followed early automatic processing, we could find evidence for *perceiving* without awareness. Similarly, in the case of memory retrieval, if we eliminated feelings like familiarity that follow a direct search process, and if the search process itself were automatic and not consciously experienced, we might find *remembering*—in the sense of accessing the record of past experience in memory—without awareness.

This may seem an unlikely possibility, but reflection suggests cases where it commonly occurs. Consider what happened when I discovered moths in the cupboard where I keep my Wheaties. I had to move the Wheaties while de-mothing the cupboard; for several mornings afterward, I found myself standing at the empty cupboard, bowl in hand, suddenly wondering what I was doing. Looking for the Wheaties, of course. I had "remembered" their former location without being aware of retrieving the information. The conscious knowledge of retrieval came only when the empty cupboard gave me some negative feedback!

This example is inappropriate for present purposes, however: It shows remembering without awareness in the sense of retrieving a well-practiced, habitual action. In this same sense, *perceiving* without awareness is a form of *retrieving* without awareness. If I am shown the word *bird* briefly, so that I don't become aware of it, we know that it may still make contact with the meaningful representation of the bird concept in my memory (see Chapter 3). That representation has been retrieved from the printed cue *bird* automatically, without my awareness. Retrieving the concept of bird and the location of Wheaties reflects access to what Chapter 2 referred to as *semantic* knowledge, learned over many experiences. It is more interesting here to consider the possibility of retrieving *episodic* knowledge (see Chapter 2)—the information encoded from a particular event—without awareness, through direct search.

It is episodic knowledge that is tested in the usual list-learning procedures of laboratory experiments. I am not asked to recognize that brickbat is a word (a semantic fact), but that the word brickbat occurred in a life episode in which I studied a list. If I were to somehow access that episode, but not have feelings that brickbat was particularly familiar, I might be said to be remembering (or retrieving) without awareness. I would be aware of perceiving the retrieval cue "brickbat," but not of remembering the earlier episode in which "brickbat" occurred.

Experimental Demonstrations—In order to demonstrate this phenomenon experimentally, we have to have some measure of remembering that does not rely on a conscious, verbally reportable end product; this rules out conventional recognition and recall measures. And, we should use an experimental task that promotes direct access to the memory representation of interest, rather than an indirect, attention-demanding process that turns up associated conceptual and contextual information as intermediate products. If the latter type of search process occurred, awareness would presumably accompany it. We want to optimize the possibility that the link between access to stored knowledge and awareness of that access is broken.

Recent work on clinical as well as normal populations suggests specific situations that meet these requirements—and, in which retrieval and conscious remembering appear to be unlinked. These situations do not require an introspective evaluation of the contents of memory in order to demonstrate that retrieval has occurred. And they use rich retrieval cues (relative to the contextual cues of recall), which should promote direct access to memory representations, in contrast to associative chaining.

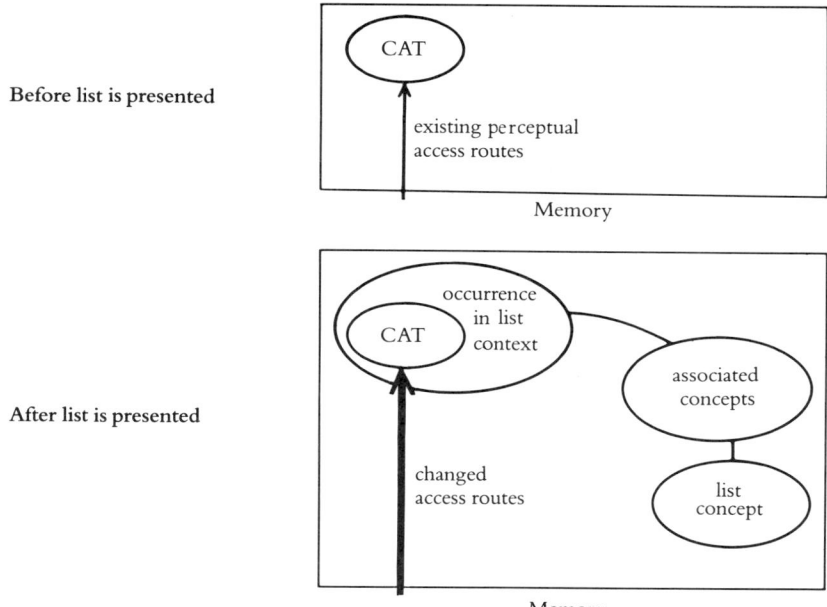

Before list is presented

After list is presented

Figure 4.2   Two results of presenting a word (cat) in a list: a change in its perceptual accessibility, and an associative structure relating it to the list context and other concepts. Both can provide evidence that the presentation is remembered.

(Note that I use "direct" here, but not "automatic." As we will see, remembering without awareness has been evidenced in situations where retrieval is effortful and presumably done with awareness, but does not follow mediating conceptual chains.)

Many tests in which there is evidence for remembering without awareness seem to have another characteristic. The memory representations that are "remembered" seem to be close to the perceptual (or motor) periphery and used in well-practiced processing activities. The evidence for remembering in these tasks is actually provided by demonstrated changes in these activities.

The situation may be something like Figure 4.2, a revised version of 4.1. Here we see that the presentation of a word like cat has multiple effects on memory. It sets up an episodic representation in association with other information (also depicted in Figure 4.1), and it changes memory representations along the perceptual pathway from the word cat to the corresponding cat concept. Thus it changes the search process that accesses the concept when the word is given as a cue. We can now find evidence that the occurrence of *cat* is remembered through different testing procedures: those that tap the internal representation of the concept cat (and associated information) and those that tap the direct-access route from the word to that representation. The latter procedures may provide evidence for remembering without awareness.

An excellent candidate for a task that promotes direct access to memory representations and measures memory without requiring awareness is the perceptual-identification procedure used by Jacoby and Dallas (1981). Here subjects try to read briefly presented and masked words; they do not have to report remembering the words from a list. Yet this task can also provide a measure of remembering as follows: when briefly presented, masked words are viewed, there is a certain average percentage that are identified. But if these same words were recently seen as part of a list, the percentage identified under brief, masked viewing conditions is higher. Thus the difference between identification in these two conditions (haven't been seen recently/just shown on a list), or the "perceptual-identification gain," is an indication of the effects of the list presentation on memory. The greater the gain in perceptibility due to having recently seen these words on a list, the more the list presentation must have affected memory.

The kind of experiment that uses such memory measures to demonstrate remembering without awareness in normal subjects generally has three phases. First, subjects study a list of words. In the second and third phase they are given two kinds of tests in which the words appear—conventional recognition or recall, and an indirect test which does not demand reports about the experience of remembering. Performance in one task is broken down according to performance in the other.

Using this procedure, Jacoby and Witherspoon (1982) looked at the probability of success in perceptual identification, partitioned by whether the to-be-perceived words had previously been studied and recognized, studied but not recognized, or not studied (not in the list). They found that the percentage of recognized words that were perceptually identified was no greater than the percentage of *un*recognized words that were perceptually identified. Having seen a word in the initial list increased the probability of its being perceived—thus showing, in some sense, that the word was "remembered"—but this gain in perceptibility did not depend on awareness of remembering the word. There seemed to be two quite different forms of remembering: one manifested in aware recognition, the other in changes in perceptual processes. For the latter form of remembering, recognition was unnecessary, even irrelevant.

Another task in which there appears to be remembering without awareness again uses, as the memory measure, changes in perceptual processing—in this case accessing a word's meaning from its sound. In the relevant study (Jacoby & Witherspoon, 1982), there were again three phases: subjects first heard a homophone (word-sound with more than one spelling) in the context of a question that biased its less frequent spelling (as in, "What instrument uses a *reed*?"). In the second phase, subjects spelled homophonic words, given an oral presentation. In the third, they took a recognition test on the initially heard words. This task provides two measures of memory for the words heard in phase one: recognition performance, and a measure of "spelling bias" from the second phase. The latter reflects a tendency to spell a word with the infrequent spelling that had been biased in the first phase. The subjects did show an increased tendency to spell a word with the less frequent spelling when it had been biased initially, indicating that they had some memory for the word's prior occurrence. However, their ability to recognize words that they spelled in the biased way was no greater than their ability to recognize words that they had spelled in the usual way. Thus, the spelling-bias measure of memory was independent from the recognition measure. Again, as in the experiment on perceptual identification, there seems to be "remembering" that does not rely on awareness. And again, this form of remembering seems to tap changes in direct pathways from external stimuli to memory representations.

Another task in which normal subjects demonstrate remembering without awareness is one of completing words from fragments (e.g., completing A __'__ E __ IA to make a word).[2] Tulving, Shacter, and Stark (1982) and Graf, Mandler, and Haden (1982) found that prior presentation of a list was "remembered," as evidenced by greater success in completing fragmented words from the list, but that this form of remembering was independent from awareness of having a memory. For example, Graf et al. compared fragment-completion performance (completing words from their first three letters) for words that had been studied meaningfully—they were recalled quite well (30% were recalled); had been studied nonmeaningfully (during study, each word's vowels were to be compared to those of a previous word)—these were recalled at a miserable 8% rate; and had not been studied at all. Fragment completion (where a response was counted correct only if it matched a word used in the experiment, whether studied or not) was much better for the studied words than the unstudied, but *how* much better did not vary significantly with the mode of study. Fragments of meaningfully studied words were completed at a 31% rate, those of nonmeaningfully studied words at a 28% rate, and those of unstudied control words at a rate of only 6%. In other words, memory for the studied words was demonstrated by improved fragment completion, virtually the same for words studied meaningfully and nonmeaningfully. This form of memory therefore appeared to be independent of the degree of overt recall of the words, which was dramatically affected by the type of study task. Thus subjects could successfully complete a word (from "def" to "defend") but not remember studying it.[3]

This word completion task is similar, yet different from, the others I have described. To measure remembering, it examines access to the internal representation of a word from a strong cue (the fragment) which is more specific and less contextual than the general cue "Recall that list." In this sense the task is like those described previously. Fragment completion is particularly like the perceptual-identification task, in that words are to be "read" from patterns that provide incomplete visual information. Prior exposure to the words might therefore affect fragment completion by altering well practiced perceptual processes used in reading. As support for this idea, consider that Graf et al. found that fragment-completion performance was unaffected by voluntary, attention-demanding encoding processes. If viewing the list affected fragment completion by creating or altering nonautomated processes in memory, we might expect to see some impact of the way attention was deployed at the time the list was viewed. But if list exposure altered automated perceptual processing, we might not expect attentional encoding to have an effect.

Yet no one would pretend that completing words from fragments is automated and unconscious; the task differs from others used to study unaware remembering in this respect. If I am asked to complete A _ _ A _ _ IN, for example, I may consciously experiment with several intermediate "products," including *Aladdin*, before coming up with *Assassin*. Subjects in this task are not unaware of *retrieving*, then, but of *remembering*. Their memory system has been changed by past experience; they are currently accessing the record of that experience (after all, it is affecting their performance), but they often do not have any products from this access that lead them to be aware of remembering. Their retrieval efforts may be turning up products, but not the right ones.

Amnesia and Awareness of Remembering

Work on remembering without awareness in normal individuals has derived in large part from recent discoveries about patients with "anterograde" amnesia. This is usually defined as an inability to remember new events that occur subsequent to the onset of the disorder (rather than events in the more remote past, the forgetting of which is called "retrograde" amnesia). Anterograde amnesics may suffer, for example, from Korsakoff's Syndrome, which is associated with alcohol abuse. These patients generally show a minimal ability to remember recently learned information, when tested with recognition or recall. Having just seen a list of words, they may fail to recall or recognize most or all of the words on it.

While most early work on amnesics stressed their memory failures (Whitty & Zangwill, 1977), it is now emerging that they may perform as well as normals in other memory tests—as long as the test doesn't require a conscious, I-remember sort of response. (See Cermak, 1982; Jacoby & Witherspoon, 1982; Squire, Cohen, & Nadel, 1983, for reviews.) The tests in which normal subjects show remembering without awareness, as described above, are all performed well by amnescis. Although they may not be able to recognize or recall words in a previously presented list, they show a gain in perceptually identifying list words, a bias toward infrequent spellings that were evoked during list presentation, and better completion of list words from fragments. Amnesic subjects are also better able to figure out what is represented in a fragmented picture of some object if they previously saw the same picture whole (Milner, Corkin, & Teuber, 1968). In all these ways, they manifest a degree of remembering that approximates or even surpasses the same measures from nonamnesic subjects—but in measures that require them to be aware of remembering, the amnesic subjects lag far behind.

It is this remembering without awareness that is captured in the anecdote about the patient of Claparède that opened this book. For a more contemporary example, Baddeley (1982, p. 221) describes an interview with an amnesic patient who

> was invited to remember the name of Dr. Peter Muedell. . . . Although he had been told it many times, he was very reluctant to guess even when given the sound of the initial syllable "moo." When pressed however, he produced the correct answer with the statement that "It was a pure guess, but what else could go with moo?"

RETRIEVING VS. CONSCIOUS REMEMBERING

In summarizing the results of work with normal and amnesic subjects, Jacoby and Witherspoon (1982) suggest that they support a general distinction between remembering, and awareness of remembering. To be more specific, we can make a distinction between retrieving (or accessing) stored information and awareness of remembering. The latter requires not only that information be accessed, but that one be aware of that access. Awareness is not,however, an inevitable consequence of retrieving.

The experiments just described make clear that the occurrence of information in the sensory world can change the memory system that received that information in various ways—only some of which give rise to the conscious experience of remembering, once the occurrence is retrieved. The initial occurrence can alter subsequent processing that directly accesses the same memory representation. This may produce "remembering without awareness"—measurable effects in some tests of memory, but not others that require an overt memory report. The initial occurrence of some item can also produce (for nonamnesics at least) a conscious product, like a heightened feeling of familiarity, when the item recurs—an effect that is observable in a recognition test. This may lead to awareness of remembering, though not of searching memory. Finally, the initial occurrence of an item can produce an associative structure in memory, interconnecting some representation of the item with representations of the context in which it occurred and related concepts. This effect will be evident in recognition and recall tests, and it can produce awareness of memory search as well as of remembering.

These various effects may have considerably different time courses. Familiarity effects, as measured in recognition tests in the laboratory, appear to decline rapidly in the interval after an item is presented (Mandler, 1980, p. 254). This contrasts with the effects of presentation on some memory measures that do not require conscious remembering; these can persist without a decline for some time (Jacoby & Dallas, 1981; Tulving et al., 1982). Associative structures are well known to be vulnerable to interference resulting from the formation of competing pathways, again leading to relatively rapid forgetting (see Klatzky, 1980).

I have suggested that with normal subjects, when information about past experiences is accessed without awareness of remembering, that information plays a role in perceptual processes directly linking sensory stimulation to memory representations. Although subjects may be aware of the retrieval effort, it seems critical that retrieval be direct, in the sense of not uncovering certain intermediate products—other concepts and contexual information related to the remembered information that might be used to produce a decision that something is being remembered.

Amnesics, like normal subjects, demonstrate remembering without awareness through tasks that do not use indirect, general cues. On the other hand, it is becoming clear that not all tasks in which they show they remember are ones in which automated processes change due to some experience (see a listing in Moscovitch, 1982). These subjects can learn new skills, not just modify existing ones, and early in the course of learning, processing is unlikely to be automated. Amnesics improve at reading mirror writing after only limited practice (Cohen & Squire, 1980). They similarly improve at solving mathematic series-completion problems, that is, generating a new number in a sequence by applying some rule to the numbers already present—although they don't remember learning the rule (Wood, Ebert, & Kinsbourne, 1982).

One generalization applied to the kinds of things for which amnesics show memory is that they are "knowing how," rather than "knowing that"; they use "procedural" rather than "declarative" knowledge (e.g., Moscovitch, 1982; Squire et al., 1983). This claim may seem inconsistent, however, with the view (Anderson, 1982) that early in its development, knowledge about a skill is declarative. Since amnesics show memory for potentially skilled activities early in learning, we have to assume that some elements of procedural knowledge are established very early, allowing initial experience with the task to be remembered. "Remembering" in this case takes the form of accessing the previously acquired procedural knowledge and using it to perform more effectively when the task recurs.

KNOWING, BUT NOT KNOWING

In addition to the distinction between knowing *how* and knowing *that*, we can make other distinctions which separate remembering from forms of awareness. One is between knowing *that*, but not knowing *where* or *when*. Who has not experienced seeing a familiar face, but not remembering the context from which it is familiar? This phenomenon is a step removed from automatic retrieval without feelings of familiarity. It seems to reflect familiarity, without associations to a context for the familiar item. One of the theoretical bases for recognition is present, but not the other.

And going further still, we may be aware of knowing that some event occurred previously, and knowing *where* or *when*, but not knowing details of *what*. Again, this is a common experience. We may know *that* a familiar face has changed, but not *how*. Did Jerome shave his beard, or remove his glasses, or forget his toupee? In experiments, I have found that some details of previously seen faces (like the hairline or the open/closed configuration of the mouth)—that subjects remember seeing—are recalled no better than would be obtained by guessing.

These forms of knowing, but not knowing, bring us to the topic of epistemic awareness, knowing what we do and do not know. This ends my discussion of awareness of memory retrieval, in the sense of retriev-*ing*. Most of the arguments follow fairly directly from ideas in Chapter 2. Retrieving, like any activity in the here and now, is assumed to come into awareness to the extent that it requires attention. I have argued that some aspects of retrieval fit this criterion, while other do not. We can have retrieval without awareness, or effortful, attention-demanding access to memory.

In the next chapter, I turn from retrieving to what is retrieved; awareness of the contents of memory as it results from the retrieval process. I assume this epistemic awareness reflects the outcome of decisions that are based on information accessed during earlier stages of retrieval.

FOOTNOTES

[1] A word of warning: Do not confuse *memory* recognition of this sort with the perceptual process called *pattern* recognition, as described in Chapters 2 and 3. Where it seems necessary, I will refer to the perceptual link between a stimulus and its memory representation as "perceptual" or "pattern" recognition, and the procedure of saying whether an item was in a previously learned list as "memory" recognition, or simply as "recognition."

[2] If you fail, you might try again after completing the chapter.

[3] At this point, I have presented two kinds of evidence for the existence of two underlying memory operations. One is the finding that some manipulated variables, like the meaningfulness of a study task, affect one memory measure substantially and another virtually not at all (or substantially but in the reverse direction). The other finding is that the percentage of items for which there is success on measure 2 is no greater, considering those for which there was success on measure 1, than considering those for which there was failure on measure 1. There is some reason for caution in using the latter type of evidence to infer two different forms of memory (e.g., Hintzman, 1980). It is possible to find that two measures are independent in this latter sense by artifact. For example, some stimuli could reliably show an increased probability of success on Test 2 given success on Test 1, whereas others could show the reverse trend, with the end result showing no relationship when the items are pooled to compute the percentages.

5

Awareness and Memory Retrieval: "Epistemic" Awareness of the Contents of Memory

The last chapter considered awareness of the process of retrieving information from memory. Here we will look at what this process makes possible, namely, an awareness of what knowledge is stored in memory. This awareness—knowledge about knowledge—I refer to as "epistemic" awareness or "metaknowledge." There are several kinds of self-knowledge to include in epistemic awareness: awareness of what one knows, of how one came to know it, and of how well one knows it. The principal assumption of this chapter is that all of these forms of self-knowledge originate in the retrieval process. One's stated awareness of the contents of memory is the result of decision processes which act on the basis of retrieved (cued and searched-for) information.

In this chapter I will describe and cite evidence for various forms of epistemic awareness, and will indicate the retrieved information and decision processes from which it might be derived. The topic of awareness being what it is, I could also consider how aware we are of the retrieved information and decision processes that lead to our being aware of the contents of memory, but this regress must end somewhere. Besides, I've said enough about awareness of the products of retrieval in Chapter 4, and there is not a great body of research on an individual's awareness of his or her decision processes in memory retrieval situations. So, the topic of this chapter becomes what we know about our knowledge and how we know it.

For preview, consider what we may know about our own knowledge. Chapter 4 emphasized the full-fledged "I remember" state, in which we know—or don't know, as in remembering without awareness—what we have stored in memory (as indicated by our ability to recall or recognize it). But this state is just one of many possible types of knowledge about stored knowledge. Accompanying the "I remember" phenomenon may be feelings of confidence in the accuracy of remembering. I may retrieve George Washington and William McKinley as Presidents of the United States, and may have a full-fledged feeling of knowing about both, but there is a decided inequality in my degree of confidence. I KNOW that I know Washington, but I just think that I know McKinley. Ratings of confidence modulate the I-remember state.

Another kind of metaknowledge is knowing where remembered data come from, for example, whether some known "fact" is the result of experience or imagination. And here, too, there can be varying degrees of confidence in the knowledge about knowledge.

Even in cases where the retrieval process doesn't culminate in successful recall or recognition, we may still be aware of something about the to-be-retrieved contents of memory. We may have feelings of knowing about even unreportable information. And there is knowing that we don't know. All these forms of metaknowledge are subject to change over time and events.

THE I-REMEMBER STATE

I have said much about this form of metaknowledge in previous chapters. By way of brief summary, there appear to be different types of retrieved "products" that can lead to the decision that something is known. These include a feeling of familiarity on a recognition test and associations between the representation of a retrieved item and other, related knowledge. After presentation of a list of words, we might recognize "brickbat" on a test because it seems familiar, but we might recognize "furniture" because we remember thinking of the furniture in the particular room in which the word list occurred. We can see these same sorts of bases for retrieval in more natural situations, as well. If someone asks, "Have you ever heard of George Washington?" I respond positively on the basis of strong feelings of familiarity. A more usual test question, however, might be one in which I am asked about the familiarity of a whole fact: "True or false—William McKinley was a United States President." I may answer this one by searching for associations between McKinley and knowledge about U.S. Presidents; I respond yes through a complex chain of associations, including assassinations! Answering the same true/false question about Washington is like a hybrid of the pure-familiarity and association-to-related-knowledge situations. Since I am so familiar with the fact that Washington is a President, the entire fact might play the role of a single familiar test item, and I might respond on that basis. Or I might retrieve associations between Washington and Presidents.

Once feelings of familiarity or collections of associated knowledge have become available from retrieval processes, decisions act to produce the yes or no or item-naming response required by a memory test. There are well developed models of decision processes, perhaps the best known being a statistically based theory called the "signal detectability" model, originally drived for laboratory recognition tests. Although mathematically complex, it is not difficult in concept. Suppose we have some feeling of familiarity about some tested information (like, "George Washington was a President"), based on early stages of retrieval. The model assumes that we adopt some criterion level of familiarity, responding "true" if the test item's familiarity is higher than that level or "false" if it is lower. Errors result if false items seem familiar or true ones do not.

This model can be extended from a memory decision based on familiarity alone to other kinds of relevant retrieved information. For example (Anderson & Bower, 1972), in a list-learning task, the basis for decision about a test item might be the number of associations retrieved from memory between the context in which the list was presented and the item's representation. If many associations are retrieved, surpassing some criterion, the decision will be positive. If I encoded "furniture" on a list by relating it to the furniture in the experimental room, the resulting associations between word and room might be above some criterial level needed for me to say "true" (furniture was on my list).

More generally, tests of memory usually provide some restriction on what is to be remembered. We aren't usually asked simply, "Is X familiar?" but "Is X familiar in the particular context of Y?" Not, "Have you ever heard of Taft?", but "Was Taft a President?" The degree to which associations between item information and the specified context are retrieved thus provides (through cue and search processes) evidence on which decision processes can act. I may make a mistake concerning Humphrey on this basis (you mean someone with that many Presidential associations never made it?), or I may miss Polk (isn't that a street in San Francisco?), but the decision process will generally be effective.

We can extend the basic notions of the signal-detectability decision model beyond the situation for which it was devised (laboratory-presented lists and recognition tests), to less constrained memory decisions, including the everyday sort. In its general form, the model is widely applicable. It assumes only that when a memory-related decision is to be made, "evidence" for the decision is evaluated and compared to some standard. The nature of the evidence is not restricted, except for its origin—memory. In other respects, memory decisions might be like those made by jurors who are given testimony as evidence, physicians given X-rays and blood tests, or oil drillers with geological reports. I have been focusing on the "I-remember" type of decision, in which desired memory contents can be fully reported. But other sorts of knowledge about the contents of memory are also available, based on the preliminary products of retrieval. I will consider what we can know about memory's contents other than the fact of remembering, and from what this knowledge is derived.

FEELINGS OF KNOWING WHAT CANNOT BE REMEMBERED

Everyone has had the experience of being unable to recall something, yet knowing that it is known. For example, we often find ourselves groping for a word or name that seems to be on the "tip of the tongue." William James (1890, p. 251) described this state as ". . . a gap that is intensely active. A sort of wraith of the name is in it, beckoning us in a given direction, making us at moments tingle with the sense of our closeness and then letting us sink back without the longed-for term."

Hart (1965, 1967) captured this phenomenon of feeling-of-knowing experimentally. He used materials that were likely to be learned in everyday life (like which planet is the largest in our solar system) or that were learned in the experiment (like word-syllable pairs that were to be associated). These materials were first submitted to a cued recall test (as in, "Name the largest planet," or "Supply the syllable that goes with *house*"), in which the subject was to indicate a feeling of knowing for any items that could not be recalled. Finally, there was a recognition test on the same items ("Is the largest planet Pluto, Venus, Earth, or Jupiter?"). Hart's basic finding was that there *were* accurate feelings of knowing. When subjects indicated that they felt they knew unrecalled items, they were more likely to recognize the correct answer, relative to unrecalled items they felt they didn't know.

While the literature on feelings of knowing has documented their accuracy, it has been rather short on explanations of how we can know what we know when we don't, at least at the moment, have the ability to report it. As said earlier, it would seem that feelings of knowing should be based on the products of the initial retrieval processes, even if they do not culminate in full success.

Research has documented that we can retrieve much that is related to what we can't remember at present, which might produce feelings of knowing. In a classic paper, Brown and McNeill (1966) showed this for the tip-of-the-tongue (TOT) phenomenon. They induced TOT states in college students by giving them definitions of words, carefully chosen to be sufficiently obscure that they were hard to recall, but sufficiently common that they were likely to be familiar. When subjects couldn't recall the words but thought they knew them, they were asked to try to give a "generic" report about the sought-for word, including such things as its number of syllables, initial letter, and other words of similar sound or meaning. Recall of all these types of information was in evidence. The students could accurately report such information as some of the word's letters and stress patterns, without recalling the word itself. These generic reports also were more accurate when they culminated in eventual recall of the sought-for word than when they ended in recognition but not recall. This suggests that variations in how much associated data could be reported were related to how close the search process got to full success.

Another study indicating what can be retrieved that is related to currently unreportable knowledge is the one (described previously) where subjects tried to recall the names of obscure entertainers (Read & Bruce, 1982). Even when the name couldn't be reported, subjects could report structural information like syllables and initial letters. They could recall contextual information, associated names, facts about the individual, and associated visual and auditory images. More important to the argument that these kinds of data are used to derive feelings of knowing, this study showed a positive relationship between the amount of retrieved information and the magnitude of the feeling of knowing (as indicated on a three-point scale). The feeling that unreportable names were in fact known was positively related, in particular, to the frequency of recall of structural information, associated contextual information, and visual and auditory information.

If feelings of knowing reflect how much information about an unreportable item can be retrieved, we might expect them to vary with the conditions of initial learning. This was found to be the case by Nelson, Leonesiao, Shimamura, Landwehr, and Narens (1982). They had subjects learn paired-associate items (pairs of numbers and nouns, with recall of the noun to be triggered by presentation of the number) to varying degrees. Degree of learning was manipulated in an initial learning phase, in which the pairs were repeatedly presented and tested, by dropping items out of the sequence after one, two, or four correct recalls. Four weeks later, subjects were retested, and they rank ordered their feelings of knowing about nouns that they could not recall (to the number cues). Finally, a recognition test was given on the unrecalled items.

The most important finding of this study was that the feeling of knowing about unrecalled items was directly related to the degree of initial learning. Whatever underlies such judgments in this situation appeared to be increased with additional study opportunities. A not outlandish hypothesis is that with each presentation of the number and noun for study, concepts related to the noun became associatively tied in memory to the paired number, and that later, retrieval of these associates when the number was presented led to feelings of knowing. Moreover, the feelings were reasonably accurate: items that subjects thought they could recognize but couldn't recall were more likely to be recognized on the subsequent test, and were recognized faster. The correlation between the feeling of knowing and recognition was reliable in particular for items that were initially well learned.

While Nelson et al. were concerned with how the encoding process affects feelings of knowing, Schachter (1983) looked at effects of the retrieval process. In one manipulation of retrieval, he gave subjects a recall test on previously learned words, cueing them with one of two types of cues. "Intralist" cue words were weakly related to the to-be-remembered word, and they had been presented along with that word during initial learning. Thus, for example, *chair* might be studied accompanied by *glue*, and later, *glue* might serve as an intralist cue. "Extralist" words were strongly related to the to-be-remembered word, and had not been presented during learning. *Table* would be such a cue for *chair*. Previous work (Thomson & Tulving, 1970) has demonstrated that intralist cues are more effective at prompting recall. Presumably, this is because they provide access to the memory representation of the particular episode in which the cued word was presented on a list, whereas extralist cues promote access to the word itself. If we assume that intralist cues lead to retrieval of more episodic information than extralist cues, even when the cued word cannot be recalled, and that feelings of knowing vary with how much is retrieved, we would expect more positive feelings about unrecalled words in the intralist-cue condition. Just this outcome occurred; feelings of knowing were more accurate in the intralist-cue condition as well as more numerous.

This discussion of feelings of knowing has focused on what is known. We also have feelings of *not* knowing about things we don't know. Again, these feelings can be traced to what is retrieved, or in this case, what is *not* retrieved. Glucksberg and McCloskey (1981) showed that judgments of not knowing a fact were much faster when there was little likelihood of retrieving relevant related facts. For example, the question "How old is Bert Parks?" led to a relatively long don't-know decision, presumably because subjects retrieved some information relevant to the question— that Parks had recently been terminated as master of ceremonies for the Miss America pageant because of his age. Similarly, "Does Ann Landers have a journalism degree?" leads to a long don't-know decision, because a relation between Landers and journalism can be retrieved. The don't-know response to "Does Bert Parks have a journalism degree?" would be faster. In general, feelings of *not* knowing should be diminished, to the extent that evidence for knowing can be retrieved.

One decision process leading to an I-don't-know response has been examined in some detail by Collins and associates (Carbonell & Collins, 1973; Collins, Warnock, Aiello, & Miller, 1975), who treat it as part of a set of strategies for reasoning from knowledge that is incomplete. Collins et al. describe a computer program called SCHOLAR that makes the I-don't-know inference when neither a clear-true is known about some factual statement nor can a likely-false be inferred. The inference of I-don't-know is made, in essence, when SCHOLAR knows too little about the topic to say, "I would have to know it if it were true, so it must be false." Thus, for example, if SCHOLAR knows a lot about coffee production in South America, and if it knows a lot about Peru, and if it does not retrieve the knowledge that Peru produces coffee, it will conclude the fact must be false. (I know so much that I would know if Peru produced coffee.) On the other hand, if SCHOLAR knows little about Peru or about coffee production in other countries of South America, it will reach a don't-know response to the question of whether Peru produces coffee. Here is one scenario that indicates a direct relationship between epistemic awareness (feelings of *not* knowing) and what can be retrieved.

CONFIDENCE IN WHAT IS RETRIEVED

Feelings of knowing concern what can't be retrieved but might be known. Confidence reports are generally evaluations of what actually has been retrieved, in the form of recall or a recognition response. Not surprisingly, the relationship between confidence and the accuracy of memory report is often a positive one (Murdock, 1974). We would expect this if the same retrieved information that gives rise to an "I-remember" form of awareness also gives rise to feelings of confidence about the memory report.

It is interesting, however, that the positive relationship between accuracy of memory performance and confidence in performance is not infallible. The potential failure of this relationship has been of particular interest in legal settings, where the accuracy of an eyewitness regarding a criminal identification can't be proven, and confidence is taken to be a good indication of it (Gardner, 1933; Wells, Lindsay, & Ferguson, 1979). Deffenbacher (1980) has suggested that experiments that simulate the conditions of a crime (for example, a memory test for faces and scenes rather than lists of words) are more likely than the usual laboratory studies to find violations of the positive accuracy/confidence correlation. He goes further to propose an "optimality hypothesis", which predicts when a correlation is or is not likely to be found.

According to the optimality hypothesis, the relationship between a witness's confidence in memory and actual accuracy is likely to be positive when memory-related conditions are optimal; that is, when the events at the time of encoding, during the subsequent interval, and at the test, promote memory performance. Considering memory for visual information, confidence should be directly related to accuracy of remembering when the remembered event had such characteristics as: long exposure time to original event, familiar object being viewed, viewer's stress not too high or low, viewer expects to be asked about memory, test of memory is close in time to original viewing, remembered object has changed little between initial viewing and test, distractors on test are not too similar to original item, and so on.

In contrast, the relationship between confidence and accuracy should not be a strong positive one when these conditions are violated, according to the hypothesis. Of course, violation of these conditions is more likely in the high-stress, low-visibility, long-retention-interval circumstances of a crime than in a laboratory experiment. And in support of these arguments, a review of relevant experiments was found by Deffenbacher to reveal a marked tendency for accuracy and confidence to be positively correlated in experiments with optimal memory conditions and not in nonoptimal conditions. (As Deffenbacher acknowledges, there are potential problems with a reduction in the range of responses when accuracy is low, which might lower correlations of this sort for purely statistical reasons. But the pattern is interesting.)

In view of the assumption that confidence reflects what is encountered during retrieval, the optimality results do not seem surprising. When the circumstances of encoding are optimal, and much is remembered about the initial event, this remembered information will be retrieved and will form a basis for both remembering and assessing confidence. But when little is encoded, what can be encountered in retrieval? The encountered material may be from sources other than the original, to-be-remembered event.

This possibility is given credence by the literature on what are called "constructive" processes in memory. These are processes initiated at encoding (and to some extent, at retrieval) that go beyond the information given, to integrate it with previous knowledge, creating a construction of reality rather than an exact copy. The notion that much of what we remember is an elaboration of what occurred is not new to psychology. Sir Frederic Bartlett described just this effect in a 1932 book, now considered a classic. Construction is essential to learning and the use of language. How could we gradually assimilate knowledge about some topic without relating events across time? How could we use language if each new sentence had to be explicitly related to the one before, rather than leaving the listener to draw inferences and cross references? The problem is that in addition to its benefits, constructive processing induces a certain fallibility in memory.

A much cited series of studies by Loftus and associates (reviewed in Loftus, 1979) demonstrates memory errors due to integrating new information with old. The basic technique in these studies is to first expose viewers to an event, such as a set of slides depicting a traffic accident, next to expose them to either neutral or misleading information, and finally to test them on memory for the original event. When the misleading information is fairly subtle, viewers may show a high probability of incorporating it into their subsequent memory reports (relative to the neutral-information condition), often with high confidence (Loftus, Miller, & Burns, 1978). For example, subjects might be exposed to the question, "Did another car pass the red Datsun while it was stopped at the stop sign?" when in fact the red car failed to stop at a *yield* sign. Subjects exposed to this question, which (a) biases fairly subtle visual detail and (b) doesn't blatantly proclaim a falsehood, but rather incorporates it indirectly into a question that addresses some other point, tended to recognize the stop sign in a subsequent test more often than subjects who were not exposed to the misleading information.

If the misleading information did, however, violate some central element in the original input, such as calling a red wallet that was stolen a "dark brown" wallet, subjects were not swayed; they were actually more likely to detect other misleading information. Exposure to a blatantly misleading question actually seemed to inoculate them, as it were, against subsequent, more subtly misleading questions. Another manipulation that has been found to reduce subjects' tendency to be misled is to have the misleading information come from a noncredible source, such as the driver who caused the accident (Dodd & Bradshaw, 1980).

Returning to the main point of this section, these findings illustrate that one can mistakenly have confidence in inaccurate memories and shed some light on when it is likely to occur. As the optimality hypothesis suggests, misleading information appears more likely to undermine accuracy without diminishing confidence when viewing of the original events was nonoptimal—for example, when the tested item was not a focal point in the scene. Other circumstances are also very influential. If misleading information comes from a source with some degree of social validity, it is more likely to be included in the construction of the event. Leippe (1980) has suggested other sources of information that might diminish memory but not confidence. These include stereotypes that a person holds and labels that he or she—or some other interested party—applies to what was viewed. Integration of information from the memory representation of some stereotype together with the representation of an event that resembles the stereotype might result in the "remembered" event moving closer to the stereotyped version. Such effects have often been demonstrated in the memory literature (e.g., Arkes & Harkness, 1980; Bransford & Franks, 1971; Cantor & Mischel, 1977; Daniel, 1972). In short, the confidence/accuracy relation seems to be undermined by manipulations that impair the encoding of information from a critical event and promote construction based on other experiences. These manipulations produce a discrepancy between what actually happened and what is retrieved from memory.

The correlation between memory accuracy and confidence can also be reduced by events that alter confidence but not memory. Leippe suggests that these include memory tests that are so easy they require little discrimination between remembered information and distractors, social support from interrogators, and false beliefs in how accurate memory is generally likely to be.

AWARENESS OF THE SOURCE OF REMEMBERED INFORMATION

I recently entered a music store in Palo Alto and asked for the "white-haired woman who always handles the music." The clerk and I had quite a conversation before I realized that the white-haired woman I was re-membering works in a music store in Santa Barbara. Like subjects in experiments on constructive processing, who integrate information from original events, preconceptions, and subsequent observations, I was un-aware of the true sources of my retrieved information.

The potential for integrating information from various sources is far from surprising, as I noted above. The human mind would not be capable of learning if it treated life as a sequence of discrete, unrelated events. The ability to abstract material from multiple occurrences is an important component of intelligence. Yet, at times it may have negative conse-quences, producing an inability to discriminate between fact and fantasy, or fact and fact.

A compelling example of how sources of information are difficult to disentangle has been documented by Fischhoff (1975, 1977). Subjects appear unable to remember what they initially knew incorrectly, once they have been provided with correct information. For example, subjects who believe initially that the story of Aladdin originated in Persia, but who are told that its origin was China, often end up thinking that they were initially correct. Even when they are asked to disregard the feedback about the correct answer and remember their initial erroneous response, they claim to have originally reported the correct answer. In other words, they think they knew it all along.

The knew-it-all-along phenomenon cannot be easily dismissed as due to "demand characteristics" (Orne, 1962)—implicit demands from the experimenter that the subject remember the answer given in the feedback. Attempts to eliminate these demands, and thus release the subjects's memory for the initial erroneous answer, meet with failure (Fischhoff, 1977). It would appear that the phenomenon reflects some change in the contents of memory, so that the newly learned correct answer is asso-ciated with the subject as source, and the original, incorrect answer is forgotten.

A point of controversy is whether the original state of memory can be recaptured under such conditions. Discussing experiments in which misleading information is interpolated between an original event and a memory test, and subjects are misled, Loftus has suggested that the mis-leading information actually erases and replaces the original knowledge (Loftus & Loftus, 1980). If so, it could never be regained, and the actual sources of information retrieved from memory could not be disentan-gled.

Others suggest that memory is not erased and updated in this fashion, but that the original knowledge is inaccessible. Hasher, Attig, and Alba

(1981) were able to show, in support of this claim, that the Fischhoff knew-it-all-along effect could, under appropriate circumstances, be reversed. These circumstances were rather hard to create, to be sure. In one manipulation, subjects first rated a set of statements on a seven-point scale from positively false to positively true. They were then given feedback on half the statements. Subsequently, in one condition, an experimenter came in and exclaimed that the feedback had been reversed: answers indicated in the feedback to be true were really false, and vice versa. Finally, the subjects were told to disregard the feedback and remember their original ratings.

The results are testimony to the flexibility of memory and the tendency to "know it all along." Subjects remembered their original ratings of items quite well, when they had received no feedback on those items. Subjects who had been given feedback that was never claimed to be reversed showed the usual knew-it-all-along effect—their ratings shifted an average of .44 in the direction of consistency with the feedback (trues remembered as more true; falses as more false, than originally rated). But consider the subjects who received that feedback and were then told it should have been reversed. They too showed an average shift of .44— but this time toward consistency with the reversed feedback. Thus items claimed to be true in the initial feedback, then claimed to be false in the reversed feedback, moved toward falseness, and similiar effects occurred for trues. Subjects appeared to have shifted once, then shifted equally in the other direction when the feedback was reversed.

However, in another experiment, Hasher et al. were more successful at reversing the knew-it-all-along phenomenon. When subjects were given feedback, and then told that the feedback was wrong (not the reverse of the correct answers, but just *wrong*), they were able to remember their original ratings. Their ratings for items on which they received the feedback were no different from items on which they received none, and there was no change in their ratings over the two rating episodes—pre- and post-feedback. Hasher et al. attribute this elimination of the effect to the "shock" value of saying the feedback was wrong. This appears to have forced the subjects to retrieve information they otherwise would have "lost". If the feedback were not invalidated, they retrieved information about it and shifted their ratings. When it was claimed to be wrong, however, they used a retrieval route more similar to that which had generated the original ratings. The prevalence of the knew-it-all-along effect indicates that following this original route takes extra effort, but if that effort is expended, the original information can be recovered.

Similarly, it appears to be possible to recover the original information after the misleading induction used by Loftus. The trick is to closely cue the original encoding circumstances, maximizing the potential for accurate retrieval. Recall the example of the Loftus paradigm: subjects view a slide sequence showing a car accident in which one slide shows a yield sign, then are exposed to a set of questions, one of which assumes it was a stop sign. They then see a test pair of slides, one with each type of sign, and must pick the original. The occurrence of the misleading question is found to induce errors. This result is obtained when the critical test pair is imbedded in a random sequence of other test pairs (each with an original slide and a similar distractor); for example, when the first slide in the original sequence is tested late in the test sequence. But Bekerian and Bowers (1983) contrasted the random test with one where the test pairs were shown in an order that matched the original sequence. This nonrandom test is a better cue for the original event, and in this case the effect of the misleading information was eliminated.

In a series of studies (summarized in Johnson & Raye, 1981), Johnson and associates have examined the potential for confusions of another sort—between external and internal sources of information retrieved from memory. They call the process of distinguishing between internally generated memorial information (the result of imagination) and externally generated information (the result of perception) "reality monitoring."

The basic assumption behind this research is that results of perceptual and imaginal acts coexist in memory; memory is not continuously updated and erased. Since information from both sources is in memory, how can they be distinguished? The answer is, on the basis of what is retrieved. Johnson and Raye suggest several possible ways in which the memorial residue of internal and external processes might differ: (1) Externally generated representations will be accompanied by representations of the spatial or temporal context in which they occurred. If we meet a friend on the street, we may remember the time of day and objects on the sidewalk, but if we imagine the meeting, there will be a paucity of such context. (2) The remembered event itself (as distinct from its context) should include more sensory information if it was externally generated. The representation of an imagined siren may seem less piercing than that of a siren that was actually heard. (3) The semantic, or meaningful, information in the representation of an externally generated event should be richer and less schematic or abstract. The image of a dog may lack such information as whether it appeared friendly, playful, or anxious to chase balls, and memory for the image will be similarly lacking. But the memory of an actually seen dog may convey this information. (4) When an internally generated event is remembered, so too may be the operations by which it was generated. Because perceptual processes are in large part automated and unaware, there may be little conscious memory for their occurrence, but to the extent that imagination is more effortful and aware, there will be memory for the act itself. We may remember what was involved in imagining a dog, but not in perceiving one, and the remembered process may lead to our realization that the dog was imagined rather than seen.

Johnson and Raye (1981) described a variety of evidence for these theoretical ideas. That reality monitoring can be performed is well established. In everyday life, we have relatively little trouble discriminating between dreams and reality. This is not to say that we can *always* discern the source of remembered information; it is a common experience to ask oneself, "Could I possibly have imagined that?" In laboratory settings, reality monitoring is fallible, but not impossible. Johnson, Raye, Foley, and Foley (1981) gave subjects words and had them generate others; for example, they instructed them to generate a word that began with the same first letter as a given one. In a test a week later, the subject correctly identified the source of the words (which ones were given and which invented) at levels about 70% correct.

There is also more direct evidence that the kinds of information listed above—contextual, sensory, semantic, and operational—are used in making decisions about the source of remembered information. Subjects explicitly reported using sensory cues (I remembered your pronunciation) to decide that an item had been externally presented, or they remembered the cognitive processing involved in generating a word. Another relevant finding is that subjects remembered the spatial location of perceived items better than ones that had been imagined in a particular spot in space, indicating that differences in contextual information are consciously available as a potential basis for reality monitoring.

VARIATIONS IN EPISTEMIC AWARENESS OVER TIME

What we know about the contents of memory is not fixed and immutable. What we can retrieve now to the full "I-remember" state may not be retrievable later; we commonly call this "forgetting." It is also possible that what we can't retrieve now we can retrieve later, even if we feel now that we simply don't know it. Who has not labored to remember the name of an old friend ("the one who always got the highest mark in Calculus; he wasn't even a math major and claimed to be taking it 'for fun'"), a city, a seventh U.S. President? Long after we stop trying, it comes to us. We read "Deer Crossing" and think "Frank Deerfield" or perhaps "Ptolemey, Pennsylvania" seems to pop into our mind.

The fluctuation of epistemic awareness which we call "forgetting" is common and much investigated experimentally. What is less common is work on fluctuation in the reverse direction, where what is not known at one time can be remembered later. The label "hypermnesia" has been applied to this phenomenon (Erdelyi & Becker, 1974). Although the theoretical explanation for hypermnesia is a matter of some argument (e.g., Erdelyi, 1982; Roediger, Payne, Gillespie, & Lean, 1982), its existence as an empirical phenomenon is well substantiated; it can reliably be produced experimentally. One essential to producing hypermnesia is that subjects be given multiple opportunities (or an extended time period) for recalling. Material that is not recalled at the first attempt may be reported later. If the amount of this subsequently recalled information is greater than the amount of forgetting of items that were recalled earlier (the movement of items from the unrecallable to the recallable class is greater than the reverse movement), the amount recalled on a late test may actually be greater than on an early one. Thus the amount of remembered information increases with time. (The hypermnesia procedure promotes this result because the repeated testing and recalling of items can have an effect like a new presentation, reducing the rate at which they are forgotten—see Roediger & Payne, 1982.)

What is responsible for this change in epistemic awareness, so that what was once thought—with great conviction—not to be available from memory becomes retrievable? Some introspective clues were offered by Kleinbard (reported in Erdelyi & Kleinbard, 1978), who used himself as a subject. He indicated that he seemed to retrieve once recallable information from a list of pictures in two ways. Cues in the environment sometimes initiated recall; for example, seeing a feather on the ground triggered the memory that a feather was on the to-be-recalled list. In the second circumstance, retrieval of a name of a picture was initiated by a vague visual impression, in which some aspect of its appearance (like shape) was represented. This information may have acted like a subject-generated retrieval cue; from the same shape several items could be retrieved (like gun, broom, and baseball bat, from an oblong).

What cues are useful for recovering previously unretrievable knowledge, where they come from, and how (and if) they are used, remains to be clarified. The importance of the hypermnesia phenomenon for present purposes, however, is more clear. It points out that epistemic aware-

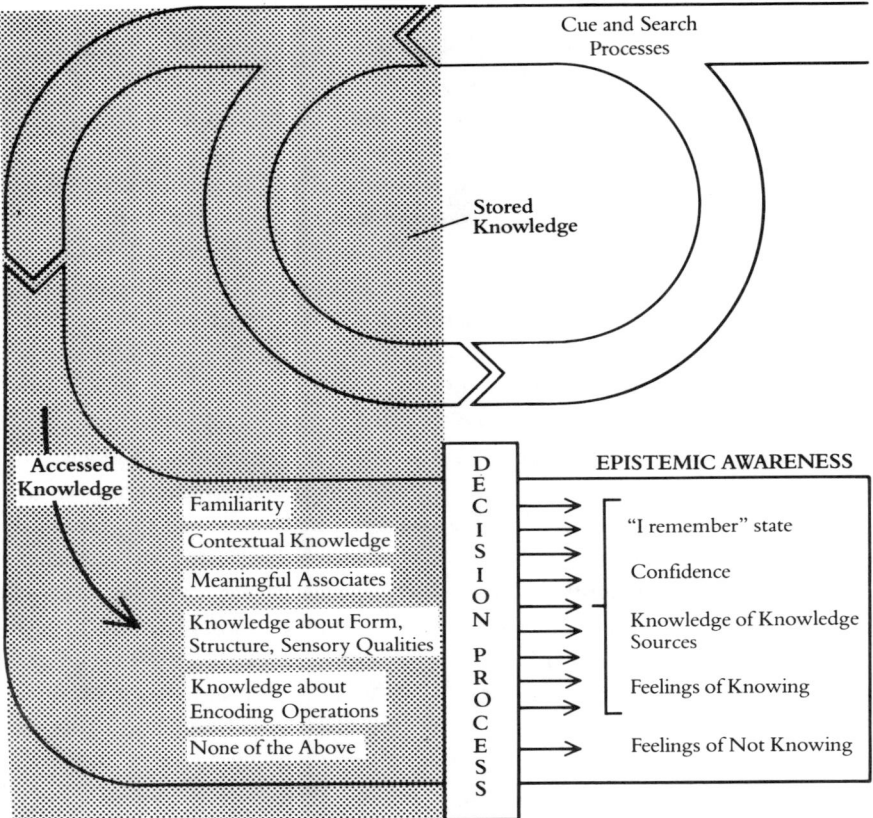

Figure 5.1   Summary view of epistemic awareness as the product of retrieval processes. Cueing and search provide access to memory information: decisions act on that information to produce awareness.

ness can change with the passage of time and the occurrence of events, both external and internal.

IN SUMMARY . . . AND SOME IMPLICATIONS

Figure 5.1 presents an overview of epistemic awareness as it has been described here. The general premise of this chapter is that knowledge about one's knowledge originates in the retrieval process, as described in Chapters 2 and 4. Cue and search components of retrieval access memory information, which is fed into decision processes that produce reports about stored knowledge. The reports come in several forms. They include not only a decision that knowledge resides in memory ("I remember"), but also feelings of knowing even when desired information cannot be reported, knowledge about where retrieved information originated, as well as feelings of not knowing. Confidence in reports can itself be reported.

The information accessed in memory that underlies these reports is as varied as the reports themselves. There are feelings that a retrieved item or fact is familiar, knowledge about the context in which it occurred and the cognitive operations used to encode it, and accessed meaningful information related to the target. Where the to-be-remembered information is verbal, like a name or a word from a list, knowledge about its sound or form can be accessed. In general, the sensory qualities of experiences can be retrieved, as well as their more meaningful aspects. Where the presence of information in memory contributes to I-remember decisions, confidence, and feelings of knowing, it may inhibit feelings of not knowing and "I don't remember" decisions, which appear to rely on the absence of such information.

Epistemic awareness is fallible and can vary over time. The "knew-it-all-along" effect is testimony to the fallibility of reports about knowledge sources. "I-remember" decisions can be wrong—even with high confidence in their being right. On the other hand, there is evidence that more concerted retrieval efforts, or better cued ones, can reduce such errors.

While I have tried to make a case for the claim that knowledge about the contents of memory is mediated by what we retrieve, I have bypassed two related questions about awareness. One is how aware we are of the products of early retrieval processes, on the basis of which we come to a decision about what we know. In partial answer to this question, I have pointed out many products of which we are aware. But whether decisions about the contents of memory are entirely based on such consciously experienced products remains unclear.

The second question is how aware we are of the decision mechanisms that use the output of cueing and search operations to arrive at knowledge about memory's contents. Nisbitt and Ross (1980) have claimed that we are largely unaware of decision processes in many instances (so that we report confabulated versions of our decisions, of which we *are* aware). Yet, to the extent that I have described memory decision processes, there does not seem to be anything that precludes our becoming aware of them. Models like signal detectability theory or the algorithm by which SCHOLAR produces a don't-know decision might not only become comprehensible but perhaps experience-able, once explained.

To the extent that we can become aware of the retrieval processes and products described here and in Chapter 4, it may be possible to improve metaknowledge. This prospect is particularly important, in view of applied areas that rely on accurate reports of what is known. Eyewitness testimony is one, as previous sections noted. Another is an area within artificial intelligence called "expert systems." In general, the field of artificial intelligence is concerned with implementing, in computers, behaviors that seem intelligent when humans do them. An expert system is a computer program that tries to emulate what a human expert does in a particular field. Expert systems have been devised to select cancer treatments, predict geological finds, and advise investors in the stock market. At the heart of the expert systems approach is discovering the underlying knowledge that an expert holds and framing it within the language of a computer program. Various methods have been used for these goals, such as having the programmer become an expert in some topic, having an expert talk to the programmer, or allowing the expert to talk to the computer itself, through an interactive program (Davis, 1979). But in any case, expert systems require that experts be able to formulate their own knowledge—that they have epistemic awareness and be able to report it.

The research findings reviewed here suggest what cognitive operations underlie such formulations, give an idea of their limitations, and indicate potential means for improving them. Research suggests that we might improve the retrieval process by attempting to access stored knowledge many times, in various ways. We should use related information that arises in these efforts as a further cue, and should evaluate it to determine the sources of remembered information, its likely accuracy, and the potential for further retrieval success. Although these strategies cannot guarantee the achievement of epistemic awareness, they should promote it.

6

Personal Models of Memory

At virtually every social occasion where I am introduced as a "psychologist," I can expect the following sort of interaction:

Other person: "Oh, a PSYCHOLOGIST! Well, (titter), don't analyze ME!"

Me: "I'm not that kind of psychologist; I don't study individual cases, like a clinician. I study people in general."

Other person (more tentatively): "What do you study about people?"

Me: "My field is human memory."

Other person (more assertive again): "Oh, well then, you should study me. I have a terrible memory for _____. I can never remember _____. I'm getting older, too. My memory is failing. How can you help me remember?"

At this point I draw the curtain on my scenario. How I respond isn't important. (For the record, it varies from "Write things down" to a discourse on memory theory.) What is important is that as an expert, I am considered to have some special knowledge that "ordinary" people aren't privy to. The question to be considered here is what kinds of beliefs do ordinary people have about their own memories? I call this set of beliefs a "personal memory model."

By personal model of memory, I mean the set of articulable beliefs that an individual holds about the general nature of human memory and his or her particular capabilities. The model includes, in brief, "folk wisdom" and self assessment. But why "articulable"; why demand that an individual be able to express beliefs, before accepting them as part of his or her personal model of memory? This requirement is further explained below, but it essentially reverts to the argument (Chapter 1) that verbal reports are externalizations of awareness. Yes, people may know more about memory than they can state, and they may state some things they don't really believe. But statements are still reasonable clues to the contents of people's models of memory. Keep in mind that our interest here is in "declarative" knowledge—facts about memory, rather than procedures that directly implement memory-related behavior. One way to assess declarative knowledge is to have people declare it.

Personal memory models are a major component of what Flavell (1971) called "metamemory," by which he meant the awareness of memory or "anything pertinent to information storage and retrieval" (Flavell & Wellman, 1977). By this definition, metamemory is a broad topic that subsumes many other phenomena discussed in this book, including feelings of knowing and memory monitoring.

The discussion of the memory modeling aspect of metamemory proceeds as follows. I will begin by indicating some of the problems, theoretical and methodological, with assessing personal memory models. The discussion is a general caveat, which I will then proceed to ignore as I attempt to glean information about memory models in any way possible. Indeed, there are several sources of information about personal models of memory, including not only conventional (or fairly conventional) psychological research but also reports in newspapers and from other public media. Having inferred some of the content of common knowledge about memory, I will discuss the similarities and differences between folk models and empirically based models of memory. Finally, I will speculate about possible sources and uses of personal memory models.

FIRST, THE RESEARCH PROBLEMS

In finding out what people know about the general nature of memory, one is again confronted with the difficulties in determining self knowledge that were addressed in Chapter 1. These problems are particularly critical when we consider that a personal memory model incorporates abstractions, that is, general beliefs about the nature of memory and its use. As Ericsson and Simon pointed out in their discussion of verbal reports (1980), when knowledge about general principles, the "Why?" of behavior, is elicited, verbal reports may be particularly fallible because the response goes well beyond information that can be kept under attentional focus (see Chapter 1).

To make the methodological issues of metamemory research a bit more vivid, consider the plight of a psychologist who is attempting to discern someone's personal memory model. The psychologist begins with a direct approach, that is, by simply asking the person what she knows. "Write an essay on what you know about memory," says the psychologist.

"Gee, I don't know, sometimes I remember and sometimes I forget; I seem to be forgetting more lately. I can't remember faces, that's for sure. Just the other day I went to the drugstore and ran into someone in line . . ."

At this point the psychologist yells, "Cease!" Clearly the essay approach is likely to lead to a great deal of rambling anecdote as well as general principle—self assessment jumbled with theory. It is also unlikely to present an exhaustive depiction of the essayist's memory knowledge. Much of that knowledge may not be retrieved and will go unreported. Then there is the problem of articulating what is known. People may suppress reports of knowledge simply because they have difficulty formulating it.

The psychologist decides on another alternative, a memory questionnaire that probes the subject's knowledge in a directed and thorough way. "Let me see," thinks the psychologist, "I'll ask some questions about encoding, some about storage, some about retrieval." We can stop there. By formulating memory principles himself, the psychologist will shape the form of the memory model he elicits. It will hardly be surprising if the personal memory model reveals knowledge that can be divided neatly into encoding, storage, and retrieval!

Another problem is that respondents to questionnaires may base their answers on what seems reasonable rather than their actual knowledge about memory, especially if the situation implicitly demands agreement. This could even lead them to "demonstrate" inconsistent beliefs. It doesn't take a test-wise college student to figure out the demand to respond "true" to both, "Continued study on a topic is better than studying for the same amount of time, but scattered over several occasions," and "Crammed study on a topic is worse than studying for the same amount of time, but spaced over several efforts." It doesn't take a test-wise psychologist to avoid such questions, either, but more subtle biases may not be so easy to discern.

"All right, says our hapless researcher, "I'll take another approach that is less direct. I'll observe behavior, and from it, infer the underlying motivating knowledge." This leads the researcher to confront a fundamental problem in the study of awareness: What kinds of behaviors are manifestations of internal knowledge or acts of which the behaver is aware? Inferring that someone holds articulable, factual knowledge about memory from that person's memory-related behavior requires a direct relationship between the two; no gaps between knowledge and perform-ance. Unfortunately, gaps exist.

These gaps are in two directions. The literature on the development of knowledge about memory indicates that children frequently under-perform, relative to what they know and can articulate. (See reviews in Brown, 1978; Cavanaugh & Perlmutter, 1982.) This is not surprising, since having knowledge is not the same as applying it. Flavell and Well-man (1977, p. 28) likened this gap between knowledge and performance to that between moral beliefs and moral behavior, calling it a form of "original sin." This sort of asymmetry between articulable knowledge and memory performance means that probing knowledge through be-havior will miss portions of personal memory models.

A more important problem arises, however, with an asymmetry in the other direction—when behavior seems to show knowledge that can-not be articulated. In an illustrative study (Shaughnessy, 1981), college students were asked to predict which of two learning conditions would lead to superior performance. Both conditions involved rehearsal of lists of words; however, one required rote repetition of the words, whereas the other elicited meaningful elaboration of the words' meanings. In spite of the fact that they recalled better in the elaboration condition, subjects predicted that the two techniques would be equivalent. Moreover, sub-jects who were free to rehearse in any way they pleased frequently re-ported (in response to a direct question) that they had rotely repeated the items; yet they recalled more than subjects who were instructed to rehearse by rote. Obviously, the students thought that rote repetition was an effective strategy for learning and persisted in this belief despite evidence to the contrary available from their own performance. More important, they *reported* conforming with this belief and rotely rehears-ing, even though other data suggested they might not be. Brown (1978, p. 133) illustrated this same problem with an anecdote about a child who was asked how he would study a set of pictures. "He replied, without hesitation, that he would look at them; he always did that if he had to remember. Given the list, he carefully put all the pictures into taxonomic categories . . . and proceeded to scan them systematically. Asked what he had (done) to remember, he replied that he just looked at the pictures just like he said he would."

When articulable knowledge lags behind behavior, the situation is par-ticularly problematic for someone trying to discern underlying beliefs. Which should we take as an indication of metamemorial knowledge, the behavior or the verbal report? In view of the previous chapters, the an-swer should be clear—go with verbal report. We have seen a variety of behavioral measures that are not indicative of consciously experienced processing. Simply because behaviors like strategic memorizing appear to be higher-level, more "cognitive," does not mean they will come into awareness. Verbal report may fail to tap some underlying knowledge that should be treated as part of a personal memory model, and in that sense be too conservative; it may tap people's reasoned sensibilities about what *should* be true rather than what they actually believe, and in that sense be too liberal. Yet, in spite of these limitations it does seem like the most appropriate indicator of folk knowledge and self assessment. And, as we will see, I am far from conservative in what I take as "articulated" knowledge about memory.

AFTER THE PROBLEMS, WHAT?

One critique of metamemory (Cavanaugh & Perlmutter, 1982) states that a complete response to the criticism of methods in metamemory assessment is virtually unattainable. My own inclination is to agree, but not to give up the enterprise. In part, that is because the present goal is different from that of others interested in metamemory. It is not to find out what people know about memory, but to find out *some* of what people *think* they know about memory. In other words, the goal here is to identify folk wisdom, accurate or not, that people seem reasonably likely to have.

My approach is to abandon the attempt to find the "right" method that gets at the "true" personal memory model. To the contrary, I accept virtually any method that seems to offer insights into people's memory-related beliefs. I allow folk wisdom to be inaccurate and even inconsistent, as certainly it is. Nor do I attempt to exhaustively catalogue it. Instead, I try to find a subset, with the sole constraints that it be (1) interesting and (2) evidenced by some sort of verbal data.

The folk knowledge that I collect in this eclectic, largely nonrigorous, fashion, I compare to the model of memory depicted by experimental psychologists, from more conventional research sources.

THE FOLK MODEL

The general as well as idiosyncratic aspects of personal memory models are harder (by far) to ferret out than the published views of psychological theory. Yet, enough can be inferred from various sources to give us some ideas of general beliefs and the kinds of self assessments people are likely to conduct. These sources include: interview/questionnaire studies attempting to discover general beliefs about memory; interview/questionnaire studies attempting to discover personal assessments of memory-related abilities; experiments using behaviors to infer knowledge in conjunction with verbal reports; information in newspapers, books, films, and other public media; and common sayings, proverbs, and adages.

Interview Studies of General Beliefs

Many psychological studies of personal beliefs about memory look at their development in children. This is no accident; the topic of metamemory has been of more concern to psychologists who study child development than to those working on adult cognition. Much of the seminal work was done by Flavell and associates, who began with the belief that developmental differences in memory-related performance might be best understood by examining the development of memory-related knowledge. (In retrospect, the gaps between knowledge and performance that were described above have been a serious blow to this belief.)

Although the present concern is with memory models held by adults, there are still good reasons to begin with a look at the developmental literature. For one thing, studies of children's knowledge about memory can tell us about the memory models of adults, assuming that the adult models are endpoints in the developmental sequence. Another, quite different, reason for examining this literature is that developmentalists have provided versions of the memory model that they think children can attain. Regardless of whether the children attain the specified knowledge and when, these idealized versions can be taken as the researchers' opinions as to what composes the adult body of folk knowledge. They thus constitute a set of intuitions other than my own.

Flavell and Wellman (1977) provided one such description of children's ultimate metamemorial knowledge, in the form of a taxonomy that divided and classified a broad domain of phenomena. The first division distinguished two broad classes of knowledge about memory—a general sensitivity to situations that call for memory effort, and knowledge about variables that affect memory. Those variables in turn were subdivided into three groups—characteristics of the rememberer (transient states like motivation or enduring states and abilities), characteristics of the task (such as the type of cues provided by a memory test), and strategy variables (such as whether or not to-be-remembered items are rehearsed).

An extensive body of research has been dedicated to verifying this map of children's potential metamemorial knowledge and studying its acquisition (see Flavell, 1978; 1981; Flavell & Wellman, 1977; for reviews). The approach has relied heavily on interview studies, generally in conjunction with behavioral data. In a seminal study, Kreutzer, Leonard, and Flavell (1975) used such behaviors as predicting which of two conditions, differentiated on some critical variable, was likely to lead to better memory performance. At the same time, they probed for their subjects' underlying knowledge by asking them "Why?" One item stated, "If you wanted to phone your friend and someone told you the phone number, would it make any difference if you called right away . . . or if you got a drink of water first? Why?" This item assesses knowledge about forgetting over time and intervening activity, and in doing so, it elicits a declarative response.

Flavell and Wellman reviewed the Kreutzer et al. data and other work available at the time their memory taxonomy was first proposed. They concluded that there was evidence for children's acquisition of both kinds of knowledge in their taxonomy—knowledge pertaining to memory-related situations and memory-influencing variables. Children appear to develop sensitivity to overt instructions to memorize, so that their behavior is different with such instructions than without. Children also develop an understanding of person-related variables like age; task variables like number of to-be-learned items, type of test, familiarity and perceptual salience of to-be-learned items, presence vs. absence of an interfering set of items, and retention intervals; and strategies like use of external memory aids and ordering search plans according to probable effectiveness. Much of this knowledge has been elicited with "Why" questions, fitting the present demands that it be verbalizeable.

Interviews with adults are less common than with children (except for self-assessment questionnaires, discussed below). This is no accident: motivating psychologists to interview children was a strong interest in the development of memory performance. There has been no similar impetus for studying adults' memory beliefs. However, more recently one motivating force has emerged: a growing tendency to use experimental psychologists as experts in the courtroom, giving evidence on eyewitness identifications. In order to convince judges that psychologists have something more to offer than common knowledge about memory, it is necessary to figure out what that common knowledge might be. Thus the interviews.

Loftus (1979) reported data from a questionnaire study of college students that evaluated beliefs about several topics related to eyewitness testimony. These data showed a majority of students giving the "correct" answer to questions about the effects of race, stress, presence of a weapon, and question wording on eyewitnesses' performance. However, few gave the required answer to a question about the (negative) effects of the violence of an event on witnesses' recollections.

Unfortunately, there is considerable disagreement among psychologists as to what constitutes a "right" answer to these questions. On some issues there are minimal relevant data. Consider the crossracial identification issue. Although several studies indicate that people are better at recognizing others of their own race than a different race, the effects are not uniform. A commonly cited study by Malpass and Kravitz (1969) shows the predicted effect (better same-race than cross-race identification) for white subjects, but black subjects from a predominantly black university actually made more correct identifications of previously seen white faces than black. (The number of *incorrect* identifications of previously *unseen* white faces by these subjects was also greater, but not enough to negate the advantage in correct identifications of those previously seen.)

McCloskey and Egeth (1983, p. 556), in a critique of the Loftus questionnaire study, proposed that "for many (if not most) variables that have been listed as suitable topics for expert testimony, either the effects . . . are not well-documented, or these effects are probably obvious to the juror." Since even young children appear to understand the effects of many common variables on memory, this point seems well taken. The problem is to determine whether there is a third class of effects, in addition to those that thoughtful adults (perhaps even children) will know even if they are not experts, and those that even researchers don't fully understand and about which they disagree. This critical third class of effects would be those that experts understand reasonably well, and thoughtful adults don't. These cases, where folk wisdom lags behind psychological wisdom, would be the ideal domain for expert testimony. The following discussion suggests areas that might fit this goal. It should be kept in mind that expert witnesses need not provide entirely novel knowledge in order to aid jurors. They can also modulate beliefs that are correct but overstated, and dispel myths.

SELF-ASSESSMENT OF MEMORY-RELATED ABILITIES

We turn our attention now to the other kind of questionnaire study mentioned above, in which adults are asked about their own abilities, rather than general memory principles. Hermann (1982) has provided an extensive review of studies that used 14 such questionnaires. (See also Cavanaugh & Perlmutter, 1982, for a partial review.) He summarizes the content of these questionnaires as follows (p. 436): "People may be asked to indicate how *frequently* they forget, how *clearly* they remember, or simply how good their memory is, how their memory has *changed*, how they *use* memory, and how they *feel* about their memory. In other words, memory questionnaires ask about forgetting, remembering, memory quality, memory change, memory use, and attitudes about memory." The actual test items are quite varied, for example, "How good is your memory for lyrics of songs?"; Rate, for frequency of occurrence, "failing to recognize television characters or other famous people by sight"; and, True or False, "I frequently use the library."

On the whole, Hermann's review suggests memory questionnaires are reasonably reliable in one sense; they give fairly stable measures from one test to a retest. Thus it appears that people's self assessments are stable. However, they fare less well on the criterion of predicting performance. The relation between questionnaire measures and performance measures is often low. Of nine questionnaires for which a validity measure relating responses to performance was reported, Hermann found that the highest reported coefficients of validity were "moderate" (over .5) for four—but at the low end, these same questionnaires all yielded coefficients from other samples that were close to zero. Thus the questionnaire studies did not make a strong case for the accuracy of self-assessment. Interestingly, this same pattern (high test-retest stability, but low generalization across behavioral situations) can be seen in measures of personality traits (see, e.g., Mischel & Peake, 1982).

Much may depend on the nature of the questionnaire and what is assesses. There is some indication, in particular, that people's self-reports of their visual/spatial or imaginal abilities are robustly related to performance. Marks (1973) developed a rather simple "Vividness of Visual Imagery Questionnaire" (VVIQ) which assesses people's ability to generate and examine visual images. Essentially, the VVIQ tells subjects what images to generate and then asks them for a self rating of their vividness.

Finke and Kosslyn (1980) used the VVIQ in conjunction with a task in which subjects imagined or actually perceived pairs of dots at various positions in their visual fields. They were asked to indicate whether they could resolve the dots separately. The ability to do so was determined as a function of dot separation and visual-field position, enabling the researchers to map out fields of resolution. Vivid imagers (as assessed by the VVIQ) were found to have similar fields for imagined and perceived dots, whereas for nonvivid imagers, the fields for imagined dots were smaller than those for perceived dots. A closer correspondence between performance under perceptual and imaginal conditions for self-rated vivid imagers than for nonvivid has been found in other tasks as well (e.g., Finke & Schmidt, 1978; Marks, 1973).

In another study relating visual/spatial ability to performance, Kozlowski and Bryant (1977) asked people to assess their own sense of direction (on a scale), then had them perform in what are often called "mental mapping" tasks. The respondents, all familiar with the university campus in which the study occurred, took part in several tasks, including pointing to one imagined location from another and drawing a map. The correlations between the self reported sense of direction and errors in pointing were fairly robust (− .40 and − .51); in addition, good-sense-of-direction subjects evidenced rapid learning of a novel route (decreases in pointing errors over repeated passages through it), whereas poor-sense-of-direction subjects showed no learning trend at all.

Hermann (1982) suggested that validity measures for the questionnaires he reviewed might have been low because the measures of performance were not similar enough to the assessed abilities. Forgetting names of colleagues is not sufficiently like forgetting lists of words to allow assessment of the former to predict the latter. The relative success of imagery and mental mapping questionnaires may reflect a closer correspondence between what is measured in performance and what is assessed.

Another important point is that the instruments Hermann reviewed asked questions about everyday life experiences, such as how often one visits a library. Thus they required retrieval of past incidents, which might be fallible. In contrast, the visual/spatial questionnaires don't necessarily require this type of indirect inference. Subjects can assess their imagery ability by generating images in the present. The VVIQ asks for just such a direct self-assessment of particular images, but a similar method might be used to assess imagery ability more generally. If someone asks me how well I imagine maps in general, I might simply try imagining one. And my self assessment should be more accurate than one based on recollection of imagery–related experiences.

Another possibility is that individuals' self-assessments are more related to performance in areas where individuals differ most widely. Perhaps there is more variability in visual/spatial ability than in the frequency of forgetting names. If so, we should be looking at people's assessments in areas where individual differences have been identified. These might include memory for faces (Woodhead & Baddeley, 1981), short-term memory capacity (Dempster, 1981) or reading comprehension (Daneman & Carpenter, 1980).

Mass Media Representations of Memory

Treatments of memory in newspapers, books, film, and television are also revealing in regard to personal memory models. There are two reasons to look at these sources: they reflect folk knowledge, and thus tell us what some of its contents might be; and they may actually shape popular beliefs. Sometimes it may be difficult to determine which is happening. If an essay is labeled science fiction, readers clearly understand it to be intended as imagination, not reality. But harder to identify is "putative reality,"—articles or fiction that make questionable assumptions about the nature of the mind, with the assumption and/or intent that readers regard them as plausible.

The treatment of memory in news and fiction seems to result in one of two kinds of stories: those in which memory performance is surprisingly good, and those in which memory performance is surprisingly bad. On the good side, there are occasional articles about mnemonists, who either by profession or hobby have acquired remarkable abilities to memorize information within a particular domain, such as names or digit strings. One such article (S.F. *Chronicle*, Sunday Punch, p. 5, 6/25/78) was titled "A man who never forgets anything." Perhaps more subtly, advertisements for memory improvement courses suggest that this kind of verbatim memorization is within everyone's grasp. Consider the following from *Psychology Today* (12/82, p. 94), under the large heading of *Instant Memory*. "Release your *photographic* memory . . . Discover your *natural* ability to recall everything."

Another topic that has received extensive newspaper coverage is the use of hypnosis to aid memory. The status of hypnosis as a memory aid is quite controversial (see below), and newspapers have aired both sides of the argument, although not necessarily equally. Martin Reiser, a psychologist with the Los Angeles Police Department, is a strong proponent of hypnosis who has been quoted (LA *Times*, Aug. 29, 1977) to the effect that hypnosis allows eyewitnesses to relive crimes rather than merely remember them, so that they are "able to look at the face and tell me how it is." To be sure, there have also been press reports airing the views of theorists who regard hypnosis as something quite different from a device for playing back a memory tape. The same paper (LA *Times*, July 14, 1982) that reported Reiser's ideas also carried, some five years later, an article titled "Research casts doubt on validity of hypnotized witnesses." This clearly expressed the ideas of those who doubt the efficacy of hypnosis in awakening lost memories, particularly the argument that hypnosis simply increases subjects' tendency to report anything, including fantasy and confabulation. Despite the reservations of some scientists, it seems clear which side of the controversy is winning in the sphere of personal memory models: according to one survey (Orne, Soskis, & Dinges, 1984), more than 95% of college students believe that hypnosis helps to expose otherwise hidden memories.

Extreme failures of memory have been aired as well as extreme successes. In particular, retrograde amnesia has been the subject of both "pseudo-real" fictional treatments and news stories. The prototypical fictional depiction of amnesia can be seen in the 1965 film *Mirage*, in which Gregory Peck played a scientist who had suffered a complete loss of personal memory. Peck was perfectly competent at speaking, navigating, and otherwise negotiating the business of everyday life—he simply didn't remember who he was. Eventually memory (and adventure) returned, emerging in dribs and drabs of retrieved experience. (Poor Peck was a victim of amnesia twice—another time in Hitchcock's 1945 film *Spellbound*.)

Real cases of amnesia have been given extensive coverage in newspapers. Cheryl Tomiczek was discovered partially clothed, emaciated, and incoherent in a Florida park in September 1980. Her condition drew national attention when she went on television to ask someone to identify her. The public focus remained over the course of a rather strange series of events, in which Cheryl was first identified by her family and taken to live with them; then rejected the family, saying she wished to be called "Jane Doe"; and still later rejoined them, even though she continued to feel that she did not know them.

In summary, the nature of memory, as revealed by newspapers and other public sources, appears to be particularly black-and-white. This is hardly surprising, given that most of us have average capacities which are worthy of neither news nor fiction. It seems that the folk view of memory promoted by these extremes is one we might call the videotape-recorder model. The major assumptions of this model are: (1) Everyone's mind retains virtually everything that impinges on the senses. (2) Individual differences are not so much in the recording process as in the playback; some people are capable of recapturing the past as if it were a photograph or an auditory recording. (3) Retrieval is an access problem, and failures to remember result from failures to solve this problem—there is no true forgetting. (4) It is possible to alter the mind by drugs or hypnosis or even appropriate training, so that a playback of the recorder becomes possible where it had failed before. (5) The mind can be altered in the other direction as well. Whole sections of the tape may be made inaccessible by physical or emotional trauma.

Not all these assumptions are captured in the examples I have given, nor do public treatments of memory consistently depict it in this way. It does seem that the general nature of this model is suggested in stories that report extreme memory abilities and disabilities. The extreme positive cases support the verbatim-record notion. And perversely, the extreme negative cases also suggest a video–recorder, although this time "on the blink." Discrete gaps in knowledge suggest discrete portions of tape eradicated. Reports of regaining lost knowledge or learning not to lose it reinforce the view of retrieval in this model—it's all there; remembering is just a matter of getting to it.

Memory Models Revealed by Adages and Quotations

Some famous quotations and proverbs relating to memory, learning, and forgetting are presented in Figure 6.1. What do these tell us about folk models? At first glance, it may seem that the most striking thing about these sayings is their frequent inconsistency. To the extent that such sayings are contradictory, it would seem impossible to glean any set of coherent folk beliefs about memory from this particular source. Even contradictory adages and quotations, however, can suggest major issues represented in folk models, if not consistent answers. Those shown reveal questions like the following: Is experience a better teacher than more conventional teaching? How accurate can memory be? What is the influence of aging on memory?

Although some adages and quotations may suggest only general issues to be addressed in personal belief systems, others may reflect the beliefs themselves. Consider the sayings about aging. Although the never-too-old-to-learn quotation suggests that memory does not fail entirely in older adults, the old-dog-no-new-tricks adage suggests that there *is* a learning deficit. Interestingly, the latter appears to reflect a common belief, that older adults have a deficit that disproportionately affects memory for the recent past, as compared to the remote past (Squire, 1974; Warrington & Sanders, 1971). In this case adages may reflect not only a general concern with aging, but particulars of that concern.

FOLK MODELS AND PSYCHOLOGICAL MODELS

We have been able to discern, from various sources, some potential content of personal memory models. The next consideration is how well folk knowledge and psychologically based models coincide. There appear to be four possible relationships between folk wisdom about human memory and inferences based on research and clinical observation: (1)

PROVERBS AND QUOTATIONS

On Learning

Learning teacheth more in one year than experience in twenty. (*Roger Ascham*)

What we have to learn to do, we learn by doing. (*Aristotle*)

In doing we learn. (*George Herbert*)

On Memory

The true art of memory is the art of attention. (*Samuel Johnson*)

A liar ought to have a good memory. (*Apuleius*)

A man's memory may almost become the art of continually varying and misrepresenting his past, according to his interests in the present. (*George Santayana*)

On Forgetting

He who has learned unlearns with difficulty. (*Greek proverb*)

The mind is slow in unlearning what it has been long in learning. (*Seneca*)

Soon learnt, soon forgotten. (*Proverb*)

Out of sight, out of mind. (*Proverb*)

There is no recollection which time does not put an end to. (*Cervantes*)

An injury is much soon forgotten than an insult. (*Lord Chesterfield*)

Let him drink and forget his poverty. (*Proverbs*)

On Aging

I am too old to learn. (*Shakespeare, King Lear*)

No one is so old that he cannot still learn something. (*German proverb*)

An old dog will learn no new tricks. (*Thomas D'Urfey*)

A man is never too old to learn. (*Thomas Middleton*)

Source for proverbs: "Proverbs, Maxims, and Phrases of All Ages." Compiled by R. Christy. New York: G. P. Putnam's Sons, 1887.
Source for quotations: Dictionary of Quotations. Collected and arranged and with comments by B. Evans. New York: Delacorte Press, 1968.

Figure 6.1   Proverbs and quotations that reveal beliefs about memory.

memory theory could be nicely congruent with common beliefs; (2) professionals could hold views that personal memory models do not represent; (3) personal models could incorporate beliefs that don't match psychological or medical data; and (4) there could be phenomena of which experts and laypersons are equally ignorant. Some of these possibilities are more interesting than others.

I have tried not only to indicate sources that illuminate the content of folk knowledge, but also to consider whether that content was accurate. Interview studies show that many beliefs about the nature of memory are shared by professionals and the general public, as indicated by children's and adult's ability to predict effects of various manipulations and to explain why they are making the predictions. Self-assessment can also be accurate, in the sense of predicting performance in psychological tasks. Treatments of memory in the mass media certainly include unbiased, scientifically sound reports.

On the other hand, the overlap between personal and psychological memory models is far from complete. Research-based understanding frequently goes beyond common knowledge. Even young children may know that more is likely to be forgotten as time passes, but empirical studies indicate that the rate of forgetting is greatest just after initial learning and declines with time. We have seen that the self–assessment component of personal memory models is quite fallible in certain domains. Perhaps most interesting, however, are areas where folk wisdom and research-based theories come into conflict. I call these "memory myths" although perhaps I should call them "exaggerations of memory," because they all have certain elements that are supported by research. Whatever the label, these seem to be cases where general beliefs and research are in less than strong agreement.

Amnesia

For the first instance of mythologizing of memory, consider the phenomenon of retrograde amnesia. The use of amnesia as a convenient literary device is commonly acknowledged. Perhaps this is what led the *New York Times* reviewer A. H. Weiler to say of the film *Mirage*, "Amnesia, which seems to disturb script writers almost as much as it does psychiatrists, is the crux of the shadowy matters only partially exposed . . . If, like the film's good doctor, a viewer doesn't take too much stock in this amnesia, *Mirage* comes off as a diverting thriller" (*NYT* May 27, 1965, 28:1).

Fictional accounts of amnesia depart from medical and psychological documentation in a variety of respects, not least of them the estimated frequency of the problem! Although common parlance may refer simply to "amnesia," the syndrome takes no single form. Major distinctions among amnesia*s* are made, based on the source and temporal nature of the memory loss. With respect to source, a general division can be made between organic amnesias, traceable to disease or physical trauma, and psychogenic (also called functional or hysterical) amnesias, which are more "purely mental" (American Psychiatric Assn., 1980). With respect to temporal aspects of memory loss, a distinction is made between retrograde amnesia, where there is forgetting of events that occurred prior to the onset of the amnesic syndrome, and anterograde amnesia, essentially an inability to retain recently presented information (presented after the onset of the disorder), without a loss in general intelligence or sense of the present. Further distinctions are also commonly made on the basis of the origin of the syndrome or the affected locus within the brain.

How does the scientific study of amnesia compare to the fictional version, in which Mr./Ms. X is shocked or beaten and subsequently forgets his/her identity while retaining the mental faculties necessary to further the plot? Although psychogenic amnesias may resemble this literary pattern, showing an extended retrograde loss that is restricted to personal-identity information, and of which the sufferer is aware (Abeles &Schilder, 1935; American Psychiatric Assn., 1980; Pratt, 1977), the organic amnesias show minimal resemblance. The literary pattern does not even consider organically based anterograde amnesias in which learning of new information is impaired. But even considering amnesias that follow head injury, the literary depiction of extended retrograde loss without an anterograde component is very uncommon (Goldberg, Antin, Bilder, Jr., Gerstman, Hughes, & Mattis, 1981). Whitty and Zangwill (1977) state that most retrograde amnesias following head injury are of *seconds* in duration. "Long retrograde amnesias always tend to be viewed with suspicion as psychogenic, and especially so when there is not evidence of severe brain injury" (Whitty & Zangwill, 1977, p. 129). Nor does the information lost in retrograde amnesia following physical trauma have to be restricted to personal identity. In a case documented by Goldberg et al. (1981), the patient forgot not only his own past history, but general information, such as the capital of France and the author of Hamlet. Newspaper accounts of Cheryl Tomiczek, the Florida amnestic patient, reported that she had to be taught such basic skills as reading, writing, and counting.

Even amnesias that appear to be psychogenic in origin do not show a discrete line that restricts forgetting to personal information. Amnesia patients may lose general information, but rapidly relearn it (Pratt, 1977). The loss can even extend to simple motor behaviors such as dressing.

Hypnosis

The common belief in hypnosis as a device for revealing "hidden" memories is another instance of memory mythology. Although hypnosis is used in criminal investigations under the assumption that it brings out otherwise unretrievable information from memory, experimental investigations that compare hypnotic and nonhypnotic retrieval situations suggest a more cautious view. Hypnosis may lead witnesses to report information that they did not report in the waking state, but this is far from the evidence needed to demonstrate "hypnotic hypermnesia," a true facilitation of the ability to remember. In natural settings there is generally no proof that hypnotically remembered information is accurate (it might be confabulation), and there is usually no control to demonstrate that hypnosis is responsible for increasing the amount reported.

In general, demonstrations of the effect of hypnosis on remembering must contrast two groups, one given hypnotic instructions at the time of retrieval and the other not, under conditions where the accuracy of retrieved information can be assessed. These requirements, though easily stated, are harder to fulfill. The two groups should be equated for the suggestibility of the subjects (which is important—see below) and the degree of motivation in the instructions (Barber, Spanos, & Chaves, 1974). Another important consideration is that subjects who are attempting to retrieve under hypnosis are often given elaborate instructions to re-experience the remembered event in fullest detail. To the extent that this "T.V. Technique" promotes self-generation of retrieval cues and increases the similarity between the original event and the test setting, performance might be improved quite aside from the hypnotic induction. Waking-state subjects should be given the same instructions, but this has not always been the case (e.g., Zelig & Beidelman, 1981). Another important point concerns the measures of remembering that are used in such experiments. Not only accurate responses but errors should be taken into account. If hypnosis does not increase the amount retrieved, but merely the willingness to report that something is remembered, both errors and accurate responses might increase (Klatzky & Erdelyi, 1984; Orne, 1979). Hypnotized subjects might report facts about some event that were remembered only vaguely and that they would not be willing to output in the waking state, but on this same basis, they might also report more confabulations and intrusions from other events. They might not only recognize more previously presented items on a recognition test, but also falsely recognize items that were not presented. This possibility has not always been considered.

From existing experiments that have considered at least some of these possibilities, there is certainly no justification for strong claims about the effectiveness of hypnosis as an aid to remembering (see reviews in DePiano & Salzburg, 1981; Sheehan & Tilden, 1983). Although some studies show evidence for hypnotic facilitation of memory performance (DePiano & Salzburg, 1981; Dhanens & Lundy, 1975), there are others which demonstrate no difference between hypnotized and waking-state subjects (Putnam, 1979; Sheehan & Tilden, 1983; Zelig & Beidelman, 1981). Those that show a positive effect generally leave open the possibility that it is willingness to make positive reports, rather than the amount retrieved, that underlies the performance gain. Hypnosis may have other, more subtle effects that are less valuable. There is evidence that it increases the *confidence* in what is remembered (Sheehan & Tilden, 1983; Zelig & Beidelman, 1981), a result with implications for criminal cases: jurors who place a high value on eyewitnesses' confidence may be led to believe witnesses who have been hypnotized simply because they are confident, and not because they are accurate.

In direct opposition to the idea that hypnosis increases the accuracy of remembering, there is some evidence that it may increase susceptibility to the effects of misleading information. Putnam (1979) and Zelig and Beidelman (1981) looked at the effects of false, leading questions posed to hypnotic and waking-state subjects during a memory test. In the latter study, subjects viewed a film showing industrial accidents. Later, either under hypnosis or awake, they were asked leading questions that assumed the existence of something that had not been present in the film (as in, "Did you see the man wearing safety goggles . . . ?", where "the" implies such a man existed). In both studies, subjects in the hypnotic group tended to answer more such questions positively.

Misleading information imparted to subjects during hypnosis may not only lead to compliant responses at the time, but may persist and affect subsequent reports about the questioned event. Laurence and Perry (1983) demonstrated this form of memory distortion by instructing hypnotized subjects to relive a night of the previous week and asking them whether they were awakened by loud noises. Almost half the subjects reported later, after hypnosis, that the suggested noises had really occurred, and they persisted in this belief even when told that the hypnotist had made the suggestion.

Studies on the effects of misleading information on hypnotized and nonhypnotized subjects are somewhat mixed, however. Sheehan and Tilden used, rather than directly leading questions, a procedure modeled after that of Loftus, Miller and Burns (1978—see Chapter 5) which introduces false information indirectly: after seeing a slide sequence that depicted a wallet-snatching, subjects were exposed either to misleading information about the crime (such as a question that incidentally assumed there had been a women's clothing store in the background, when it had been a menswear store), or to neutral information. Later, they were given a recognition test asking them to choose between statements that matched the original event, versus the misleading information. Both hypnotically retrieving and waking-state subjects were swayed by the misleading information—but to an essentially equal degree. Measures of hypnotic suggestibility (from a standard test) were similarly unrelated to the effects of misleading information. Thus, there was no evidence that hypnosis increased susceptibility to distortion (but certainly no evidence that it *decreased* susceptibility, either). However, when asked to recall the original event, high-suggestibility subjects showed a greater tendency to erroneously "recall" details that were not actually present than low-suggestibility subjects. This tendency to misrecall was not increased by misleading information; it was actually more pronounced for subjects in the neutral-information condition. These data imply there might be a general relation between suggestibility and the willingness to make positive memory reports.

Does hypnosis really enhance memory, or does it simply increase confidence, willingness to report, or even fantasy? Based on existing research, most scientists would probably say it is premature to embrace either side of the argument. As we have seen, personal memory models are considerably less cautious.

Photographic Memory

The advertisement for "Instant Memory" described above appeals to people who believe that remembering can have a photographic quality. As a teacher of courses on human memory, I have first-hand experience with how common this belief is. (Neisser, 1982, has made a similar comment.) Generally, it emerges in an account of someone, known to a student, who has the remarkable ability to call up images from memory in such detail that they can be read like a book or viewed like a picture. (There is usually a bit of envy in the description, since the images are purported to make test-taking a snap.) It is interesting that it has never been the student himself or herself who has the ability, but an acquaintance at several steps removed—a friend of a friend, an old (and long-lost) grade-school classmate.

Researchers are leery of what others accept with little question. In the psychological literature, the phenomenon of *eidetic* imagery is the closest approximation to photographic memory (see Gray & Gummerman, 1975; Haber, 1979; Haber & Haber, 1964; Leask, Haber, & Haber, 1969). It is generally studied by showing people a picture, asking them to scan it and form an image, and then ascertaining the nature of the image once the picture has been removed. An "eidetic" image is, in certain respects, a picture-like representation of the original, and "eidetikers" are people with the ability to form one. But what is a picture-like image? Lacking the ability to vicariously see the images of others, psychologists have adopted several general criteria which are to be met before an eidetic image is assumed to be present (Haber & Haber, 1964; Leask et al., 1969). Among them are that imagers should have the subjective impression that their image is located in front of them; that they are not remembering a picture but experiencing it. They should scan the image by moving their eyes around it, and the image should not move with the eyes. The eye positions during reports from the image should correspond to the positions of the reported items in the original display. The image should match the color of the original.

Isn't this photographic memory? It might be, but there are several problems with the phenomenon. One is its scarcity: despite extensive searches for people whose images meet the criteria (including publicizing the search in introductory psychology texts), candidates are extremely rare. The eidetic population is almost entirely composed of children, and even then, only about 5% of normal children are classified as eidetikers (Gray & Gummerman, 1975). Almost no adults have qualified, although there is one report (Stromeyer & Psotka, 1970) of an eidetiker with phenomenal abilities, far beyond those of child subjects (for example, the ability to call back very complex images from memory, after they had vanished). But this case lacks replication, and it is difficult to interpret or generalize from it. In contrast, in a test of normal adults (Gummerman, Gray, & Wilson, 1972) that used the more standard procedures, none were found to be eidetikers.

Studies of child eidetikers reveal another problem: it is not really accurate to call their images "photographic." Eidetic images seem to be formed in segments and vanish in segments, so that only part of a viewed picture may be represented. They do not necessarily allow for highly detailed reports, and accordingly, accuracy is not generally considered to be one of the best indicators of image ability (Haber, 1979). Most eidetikers cannot bring back the image of a recently viewed picture once that image has vanished, precluding its use to promote later recall (Leask et al, 1969). The eidetic ability does not seem highly related to other memory measures (Paivio & Cohen, 1979). In short, eidetic memory does not really fit what most people think of as photographic memory. As summarized by Haber (1979, p. 590), "It appears that the images are constructed or organized in the same way that verbal memory is, so that some visual details are omitted, others moved around, and some added. Thus, the content of imagery is also organized, and not simply an internal template or photograph of the stimulus."

All this does not mean that there is no adult with the ability to form vivid and detailed images (of something other than photographic quality), nor that there are no exceptional memorizers who make use of imagery as a memory-enhancing device. To the contrary, exceptional imagers and memorizers have been documented (see Neisser, 1982, for examples). The point is that eidetic imagery, the best candidate for "photographic" memory that we seem to have, is rare, and not all that photographic. This discrepancy between what can be demonstrated and what is commonly thought to exist puts photographic memory into the class of memory myths.

Aging and Memory

For our last candidate for memory myths, consider the effects of aging on memory. It is commonly believed that the elderly have trouble remembering events in the recent past (Squire, 1978; Warrington & Sanders, 1971), while the more remote past remains vivid and recallable. This idea is related to the saying about old dogs and new tricks, which, in implying that the elderly can't learn new things, is also implying that they remember better what they learned long ago.

Experiments on memory for events across the life span do show clear decrements with age; however, they fail to support the idea that older adults in good health (in particular, not suffering from senility) remember the past far more clearly than the present (Squire, 1974; Warrington & Sanders, 1971). Attempting to address this question, researchers have tested adults of various ages on their memory for political events, famous persons, and other information they were likely to have been exposed to for a limited and specifiable period of time in the past. Performance on recall or recognition of such information is tested in each of several age groups, and the performance measure is then plotted on a graph against the time at which the tested information is likely to have been learned. Thus we could test recognition of faces of movie stars from the 1980s, 1970s, and so on down for as many decades as desired.

If the idea that elderly adults remember the remote past better than the recent past is correct, we might expect the functions relating performance to time of learning to look very different for different age groups. Younger adults should show a usual forgetting function: the further back the time of learning, the worse the performance. Elderly adults might show the reverse: the further back the time of learning, the better the performance. At the very least, elderly adults should show a shallow forgetting function. That is, even if they don't remember the remote past better than the recent past, their greater tendency to forget recent events should particularly depress the portions of the function representing these events. Thus the difference between the recent and remote events should be minimized.

In fact, the studies just described (Squire, 1974; Warrington & Sanders, 1971) fail to support the idea of greater memory loss for recent events in the elderly. These studies do show a memory loss: the functions relating performance to time of learning are lower overall for older age groups; the elderly don't perform up to the level of the young. But, the memory loss seems to be fairly uniform across the years since learning. Warrington and Sanders found, for age groups in the 40s to 70s and 80s, normally shaped and remarkably similar forgetting functions. Figure 6.2 shows their results for one test, which indicates the more remote events were remembered more poorly for the elderly much as for the younger adults. Squire (Experiment 1) found a rather unusual forgetting function, in which performance for intermediate times of learning was highest, but the shape was similar for all age groups except the youngest. This suggests that the items selected to represent different times of learning were also different in their intrinsic memorability, but not that the elderly forget differently from the young.

At least in studies of memory for these public categories of events, the idea that the remote past is preserved in the memories of the elderly does not seem to be supported. Whoever claims that "old dogs" have difficulty learning and remembering new tricks should consider that they might also have difficulty in remembering the old ones.

WHENCE COMETH FOLK WISDOM?

Where do personal memory models originate? This is one version of a more basic question about the reasoning and inferential processes that

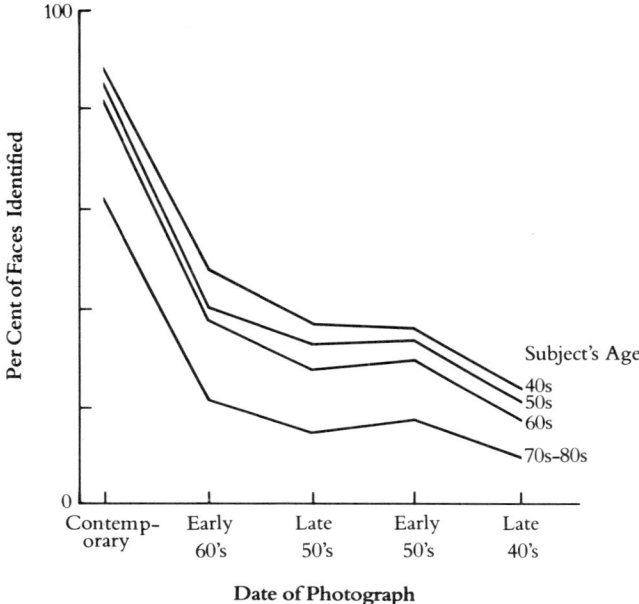

Figure 6.2 Percent correctly identified photographs of persons who were prominent at a particular time in the past, by four age groups (From Warrington & Sanders, 1971).

establish new "facts" in memory. These processes can be characterized as beginning with some set of mental representations (initial beliefs and related knowledge) and some "data"—premises being stated to the reasoner, information the reasoner retrieves from memory on the basis of explicit cues, perceptually available information—and from these starting points, by reasoning processes, deriving new mental representations—conclusions; new beliefs.

When the beliefs being established are part of a personal memory model, there are many potential sources of data. There are observations of one's own behavior and the behavior of others. Direct statements by teachers and acquaintances constitute part of the data base. There are also descriptions of memory in more public sources, such as books and newspapers. The person who is establishing a memory model has available much the same sources that I used in attempting to figure out the general content of such models.

Not only are there many sources of data, there are also many reasoning processes that can be applied to the data to add beliefs to personal models of memory. Psychologists classify these processes under such labels as

inductive and deductive reasoning, concept formation, hypothesis testing, and prototype abstraction, among others. The decision processes
described in Chapter 4 are a type of reasoning, as are the "constructive"
processes of Chapter 5. The formation of new representations by means
of these processes is studied in every area within experimental psychology: there are social inferences and personality inferences as well as cognitive inferences; there are developmental changes in reasoning and individual differences.

Theories of human reasoning and inference often emphasize how ra-
tional, accurate, performance occurs. In contrast, the potential *fallibility*
of inferential reasoning has been given greater stress by Nisbett and Ross
(1980), who trace many errors to the two strategies first described by
Tversky and Kahneman (see Chapter 2), the "availability" and "representativeness" heuristics. Recall that the availability heuristic is a guide-
line for judging how frequent or likely events are; it states that the re-
trievability of those events from memory, or their accessibility to
imagination or perception, are good indications of frequency. The representativeness heuristic is used in assigning objects to categories; it says
that an object should be judged a category member to the extent that it
resembles the categorical norm. To these heuristics Nisbett and Ross add
the principle of "salience," which states that more vivid information is
given more weight in inferential reasoning, possibly because it tends to
be more available in memory. It is assumed that application of these
heuristics is "generally automatic and nonreflective and notably free of
any conscious consideration of appropriateness" (Nisbett & Ross, 1980,
p. 18)—and in this nonreflective application lies a problem.

The availability and representativeness heuristics are often excellent
devices that lead to accurate reasoning. This is what leads to their being
heuristics in the first place. However, the nature of heuristics is that they
are general guidelines, not hard-and-fast rules that guarantee success. As
such, they will be fallible in cases where misapplied. The availability
heuristic will fail, state Nisbett and Ross, if the frequency or likelihood
of an event is not correlated with its perceptual or cognitive availability.
Vivid, available memory for a rare but salient event might inflate estimates of its likelihood. Or consider the case of unemployed workers
who overestimate the unemployment rate because in the unemployment
line, other jobseekers are so available for viewing.

Similarly, if representativeness is not a good indicator of category
membership, use of the representativeness heuristic will lead to error.
To this can be attributed the common tendency to believe that randomly
generated sequences that look regular, like 12345, are not really random.
Although this sequence is as likely as any other of five digits, it is not

representative of the output of a random number generator and is therefore rejected as nonrandom (Nisbett & Ross, 1980).

It is not difficult to draw a connection between the availability and representativeness heuristics and common myths about memory. Newspapers may distort people's views of memory while remaining completely factual, because they make unusual memory abilities available to their readers through articles and news reports. Unusual memory abilities or impairments are likely to be vivid and therefore more memorable; their vividness is why they become "news". Through the availability heuristic, estimates of the frequency of exceptional memorizers or odd memory losses may be inflated.

The availability and representativeness heuristics may also play a fundamental role in beliefs about aging. One outcome of the representativeness heuristic, according to Nisbett and Ross (Chapter 5), is a tendency to explain one effect by looking for causes like those of other, similar effects. Aging does "cause," or at least correlate with, general losses in memory performance (but not predominantly for the recent past). Faced with any particular memory loss, such as misplaced house keys, an older person may be inclined to attribute it to aging. There may be a tendency to blame all lapses of memory on aging, merely because age does produce some memory deficits. The availability heuristic can be misused here as well. If memory lapses are salient events, the elderly may overestimate the frequency with which they occur. Even more important, the elderly may assess their memory by comparing recall of mundane occurrences in the present to vivid, much recalled and rehearsed experiences from the past. The good memory for past experiences will be overestimated by virtue of their availability, and the result will be a belief that memory for the recent past is worse than for the remote past.

The use of heuristics is part of a more general need for economy in information processing. Rules of thumb are valuable because they reduce the need to gather and evaluate large amounts of data; one trades speed and ease for a degree of inaccuracy. The user of heuristics is like an insurance company that penalizes the particularly healthy in an age group and is overly generous to the infirm, by using the average, not-so-healthy person to set rates. Another manifestation of the same economy drive is a tendency for the memory system to represent information in stereotyped or normalized form. This tendency can be seen in many guises in the psychological literature. Memory for locations in maps tends to move them toward alignment in a straight line and to rotate them into congruence with the usual North/South, East/West axes (Tversky, 1981). This normalization leads to such errors as thinking that San Diego is due South of San Francisco (it is considerably East) or that Washington is at the same latitude as Maine. It has been proposed that stereotypes or prototypical representations in memory function in a wide variety of human activities. When we enter a restaurant, we take advantage of a stereotyped restaurant procedure that leads us to seat ourselves in a fast-food outlet and wait for the maitre d' in a three-star restaurant. We use representations of the general nature of stories to follow the text of any particular tale, despite gaps and presuppositions. Authors incorporate these gaps, knowing that our story prototypes will help us to accommodate to them. We categorize people in stereotyped ways, in part in order to predict and comprehend behaviors (Cantor, Mischel, & Schwartz, 1982).

The idea that memory is like a videotape recorder, which seems to manifest in beliefs about photographic memory and exaggerated ideas of the effects of hypnosis, is also a stereotype. Loftus and Loftus (1980) suggest that publication of radical views about memory contributes to this stereotype. They cite in particular widely disseminated reports (not only in newspapers, but textbooks) of a body of work by Wilder Penfield (e.g., 1969). Penfield described epileptic patients, whose brains were being electrically stimulated as part of a surgical procedure, as producing "experiential responses," during which they felt they were actually hearing sounds or viewing scenes. On this basis he theorized that all of past conscious experience lay latent in the brain, awaiting only the appropriate probe to reawaken it. Others, however, have strongly disagreed. At the outset, it is questionable to assume that people are "remembering" under these conditions, rather than fantasizing (and some reports suggest the latter). Neisser (1967) pointed out that the "experiential" responses were not like awakened and re-perceived events, but more abstract and dream-like; more like thought than hallucination. Loftus and Loftus (1980, p. 414) also state that these responses were extremely infrequent: ". . . less than 3% of the patients contributed the lifelike experiential responses for which Penfield's work is so famous."

Although people's models of memory can be inaccurate, in part by virtue of stereotypes and heuristics, we have seen that beliefs about memory can be "common sense" as well; they can coincide with findings from controlled research. Even in memory "myths" there are elements that are supported experimentally. Although the aged may not forget selectively (at least, public events), they do show decrements in remembering. And although hypnosis may not dramatically enhance the ability to remember, it does affect memory performance (potentially in negative ways). Memory myths are a mixture of fallibility and sensibility, and thus, so too are personal models of memory.

7

What Are We Aware of about Awareness and Memory?

As stated in Chapter 1, the goal of this book was to outline an emerging area within the information-processing approach to human memory, concerned with the relationship between memory and awareness. The topics covered can be summarized as the *content* and *origins* of awareness—what we are aware of, and how we come to be aware. The basis for the depiction of awareness was largely experimental, with some sorties into clinical research.

Given the youthful state of the study of awareness within the information-processing approach, this book attempted more to organize and illustrate than to theorize. I have suggested that the research topics that constitute this area might be loosely partitioned by distinguishing among three types or levels of awareness. An important difference among these levels is their content. "On-line" awareness is consciousness of ongoing mental activities and their immediate products. In the perceptual domain, it is thought to occur relatively late, so that we are aware of perceiving relatively high-level or abstract representations; this means that much perceptual processing occurs without awareness. In the motor domain, or considering performance in general, awareness has been associated with control structures that set goals and monitor performance; the level of these structures presumably moves upward as skill develops. On-line awareness was also considered in the context of memory retrieval, and it was proposed to accompany effortful associative search processes. The absence of on-line awareness of retrieval is manifested in the phenomenon of remembering without awareness. "Epistemic" awareness is cognizance of accessible knowledge at some point in time, confidence that what is accessed accurately reflects past experience, feelings of knowing and not knowing—in short, knowledge about knowledge. "Personal models" of memory constitute the third type of awareness, a sensibility about memory as a general system and an appreciation of one's own abilities in relation to that system. An important question about on-line awareness concerns its presence or absence. The question more often asked about the latter two types of awareness is whether they are accurate or inaccurate. As we have seen, the answer to the question about accuracy is, sometimes yes, sometimes no. Epistemic awareness suffers when conditions of encoding into memory are inadequate to provide a body of knowledge for retrieval and assessment, and personal models can err when sources of information about memory are exaggerations or distortions.

I have used the term "levels of awareness" for these phenomena because they appear to result from different degrees of intermediate or inferential processing. On-line awareness is assumed to be associated in a direct way with ongoing attention-demanding processes. Epistemic awareness, I have suggested, is acquired through retrieval processes that access information in long-term memory, then operate on that information to produce decisions about what is or is not known. Finally, personal models of memory are in large part the product of complex reasoning processes, potentially integrating information from a variety of sources.

The experimental methods and measures on which these views of awareness are based are quite varied. For example, the distinction between attentional and automatic processes, so critical to the notion of on-line awareness, has been studied with measures of response time, skin reactions, and verbal reports. Motor skills have been measured with the time to make simple movements and the intertone intervals of professional pianists playing Bartok. As important as *what* is measured is *how* measures vary predictably under critical manipulations. The manipulated variables that have been discussed include associative relatedness, conceptual similarity of linguistic utterances, number of to-be-detected targets and simultaneously performed tasks—the list goes on. In short, the machinery of the information-processing approach has been brought to bear on this theoretical distinction, as on others.

At the heart of the study of awareness itself is verbal report, which has appeared here in such guises as reports of perceived and recalled items, statements about feelings of knowing and about memory-related beliefs, confidence ratings, and introspective reports of ongoing retrieval processes, among others. As indicated above, the method for studying awareness does not consist merely of obtaining a verbal report about some task performance or body of knowledge. Verbal responses are evaluated under various experimental manipulations, in tests of specific predictions. Consider the study of epistemic awareness where measures include recognition and recall responses, feelings of knowing, and confidence ratings. The manipulated variables described in Chapter 5 encompass encoding conditions (like number of presentations), retrieval conditions (recall cues), events during the retention interval (interpolated information, misleading or neutral), and the nature of the experimental stimuli themselves.

In addition to examining a particular type of verbal report under various conditions, several types of reports can be compared. Feelings of knowing about some target information in memory can be evaluated relative to ultimate recognition or recall of the target and to recall of related information. Statements about memory-related beliefs can be compared to the respondent's memory performance and predictions about the performance of others. Perceptual identification can be contrasted with memory recognition. Another technique is to translate reports about information-processing activities into experimentally manipulable variables, making more direct tests a possibility.

Now that we have learned something about what awareness is and how it is studied, what good is it? Previous chapters have given some specific hints at applications of this research, and a general theme as well. Awareness is selective; what we are aware of can come under some degree of control. Psychodynamic theories have emphasized the importance of awareness and the control that it makes possible over clinical symptoms. Memory theories should adopt a similar view: if we can understand the bases for awareness of memory-related activities, our ability to control (or decontrol) them might be increased.

To improve our ability to know what we know, for example, we might focus on the retrieval process. We assume that there can be controlled, attention-demanding search processes; why not learn efficient ways to use attention? The devisers of memory-enhancement or "mnemonic" techniques have usually talked about methods that must be used at the time of initial learning. But there are also possible techniques for the time of retrieval. Chapters 4 and 5 suggest that retrievers might learn devices for generating cues based on initial products of the search process, resembling those products in sound, form, or meaning. People might learn devices for guiding associative search; for example, deliberately attempting to retrieve events in the order in which they occurred, or considering the features of stereotypes when trying to recall specific instances.

Awareness of personal memory models might also lead to improvements. People can be informed about incorrect beliefs, which might lead them to revise their models. They can be informed about the sources of beliefs and the likelihood of their being reliable. Along these lines, Chapter 6 attempted to make readers aware of inaccurate beliefs about memory and the sources from which they might stem.

In the case of on-line awareness, a common goal is to lose control rather than gain it (or at least move the site of control upward in a hierarchy). Pianists would generally prefer not to devote attention to each finger; readers want to get the message rather than the medium. We assume that skills in piano, reading, or virtually any cognitive, perceptual, or motoric domain result from practice. What is needed is to determine practice routines that automate performance, or that prevent automatization where that is desired—after all, proofreaders *want* to catch spelling errors!

The ideas of William James about the uses of awareness are in this, as in other matters, remarkably cogent. (James lacked the experimental techniques available to psychologists a century later and expressed disdain for the existing experimental method, but he never lacked ideas.) In Chapter 5 of his *Principles of Psychology* (1890), James wrote about the potential usefulness of consciousness in reaction to an alternative view, which he called the "conscious automaton theory." As expressed by Huxley and quoted by James (p. 131), this view stated:

> The consciousness of brutes would appear to be related to the mechanism of their body simply as a collateral product of its working, and to be as completely without any power of modifying that working as the steam-whistle which accompanies the work of a locomotive engine is without influence on its machinery . . . It is quite true that, to the best of my judgment, the argumentation which applies to brutes holds equally good of men . . . that in men, as in brutes, there is no proof that any state of consciousness is the cause of change in the motion of the matter of the organism."

James, however, argued strenuously against the conscious automaton, claiming that consciousness was "efficacious" by virtue of its being a "selecting agency." What it selected, said James, were those activities that were advantageous to the organism, and that were nonhabitual or unstable—and thus needed to be controlled. Consciousness, said James, "is only intense when nerve-processes are hesitant. In rapid, automatic, habitual action it sinks to a minimum" (p.142). ". . . the distribution of consciousness shows it to be exactly such as we might expect in an organ added for the sake of steering a nervous system grown too complex to regulate itself" (p. 144).

References

Abeles, M., & Schilder, P. Psychogenic loss of personal identity. *Archives of Neurology and Psychiatry*, 1935, *34*, 587–604.

American Psychiatric Assn. *Diagnostic and Statistical Manual of Mental Disorders*, 3rd ed. Washington, D.C.: American Psychiatric Assn., 1980.

Anderson, J. R. *Language, Memory, and Thought*. Hillsdale, N.J.: Erlbaum, 1976.

Anderson, J. R. Acquisition of cognitive skill. *Psychological Review*, 1982, *89*, 369–406.

Anderson, J. R., & Bower, G. H. Recognition and retrieval processes in free recall. *Psychological Review*, 1972, *79*, 97–123.

Arbib, M. A. Perceptual structures and distributed motor control. In V. Brooks (Ed.), *Handbook of Physiology*, Vol. 3: Motor Control. Washington, D.C.: American Physiological Society, 1981.

Arkes, H. R., & Harkness, A. R. Effect of making a diagnosis on subsequent recognition of symptoms. *Journal of Experimental Psychology: Human Learning and Memory*, 1980, *6*, 568–575.

Atkinson, R. C., & Juola, J. F. Factors influencing speed and accuracy of word recognition. In S. Kornblum (Ed.), *Attention and Performance*, Vol. 4. New York: Academic Press, 1973.

Baddeley, A. The concept of working memory: A view of its current state and probable future development. *Cognition*, 1981, *10*, 17–23.

Baddeley, A. D. Domains of recollection. *Psychological Review*, 1982, *89*, 708–729.

Balota, D. A. Automatic semantic activation and episodic memory encoding. *Journal of Verbal Learning and Verbal Behavior*, 1983, *22*, 88–104.

Barber, T. X., Spanos, N. P., & Chaves, J. F. *Hypnotism: Imagination and Human Potentialities*. Elmsford, N.Y.: Pergamon, 1974.

Bartlett, F. C. *Remembering: A Study in Experimental and Social Psychology*. Cambridge: Cambridge University Press, 1932.

Bekerian, D. A., & Bowers, J. M. Eyewitness testimony: Were we misled? *Journal of Experimental Psychology: Learning, Memory, and Cognition*, 1983, *9*, 139–145.

Blum, G. S. *A Model of the Mind*. New York: Wiley, 1961.

Boring, E. G. *A History of Experimental Psychology*, 2nd ed. New York: Appleton-Century, 1950.

Bransford, J. D., & Franks, J. J. The abstraction of linguistic ideas. *Cognitive Psychology*, 1971, *2*, 331–350.

Broadbent, D. E. *Perception and Communication*. London: Pergamon, 1958.

Brown, A. L. Knowing when, where, and how to remember: A problem of metacognition. In R. Glaser (Ed.), *Advances in Instructional Psychology*, Vol. 1. Hillsdale, N.J.: Erlbaum, 1978.

Brown, R., & McNeill, D. The "Tip of the tongue" phenomenon. *Journal of Verbal Learning and Verbal Behavior*, 1966, *5*, 325–337.

Brown, W. P. Conceptions of perceptual defence. *British Journal of Psychology Monographs*, Supplement No. 35, 1961.

Cantor, N., & Mischel, W. Traits as prototypes: Effects on recognition memory. *Journal of Personality and Social Psychology*, 1977, *35*, 38–48.

Cantor, N., Mischel, W., & Schwartz, J. Social knowledge: Structure, content, use, and abuse. In A. H. Hastorf & A. M. Isen (Eds.), *Cognitive Social Psychology*. New York: Elsevier/North Holland, 1982.

Carbonell, J. R., & Collins, A. M. Natural semantics in artificial intelligence. *Proceedings of Third International Joint Conference on Artificial Intelligence*, 1973, 344–351. (Reprinted in the *American Journal of Computational Linguistics*, 1974, *1*, Mfc.3.)

Carr, T. H. Consciousness in models of human information processing: Primary memory, executive control and input regulation. In G. Underwood & R. Stevens (Eds.), *Aspects of Consciousness*, Vol. 1. London: Academic Press, 1979.

Cavanaugh, J. C., & Perlmutter, M. Metamemory: a critical examination. *Child Development*, 1982, *53*, 11–28.

Cermak, L. S. (Ed.), *Memory and Amnesia*. Hillsdale, N.J.: Erlbaum, 1982.

Chase, W. G., & Ericsson, K. A. Skilled memory. In J. R. Anderson

(Ed.), *Cognitive Skills and Their Acquisition*. Hillsdale, N.J.: Erlbaum, 1981.

Cherry, E. C. Some experiments on the recognition of speech with one and two ears. *Journal of the Acoustical Society of America*, 1953, *25*, 975–979.

Claparède, E. Recognition and "me-ness." *Archives de Psychologie*, 1911, *11*, 79–90. (Translation in D. Rapaport (Ed.), *Organization and Pathology of Thought*. New York: Columbia University Press, 1951.)

Cohen, N. J., & Squire, L. R. Preserved learning and retention of pattern-analyzing skill in amnesia: Dissociation of knowing how and knowing that. *Science*, 1980, *210*, 207–210.

Collins, A., Warnock, E. H., Aiello, N., & Miller, M. L. Reasoning from incomplete knowledge. In D. G. Bobrow & A. Collins (Eds.), *Representation and Understanding*. New York: Academic Press, 1975.

Coltheart, M. Iconic memory and visible persistence. *Perception & Psychophysics*, 1980, *27*, 183–228.

Corteen, R. S., & Wood, B. Autonomic responses to shock-associated words in an unattended channel. *Journal of Experimental Psychology*, 1972, *94*, 308–313.

Craik, F. I. M. Age differences in human memory. In J. E. Birren & K. W. Schaie (Eds.), *Handbook of the Psychology of Aging*. New York: Van Nostrand Reinhold, 1977.

Craik, F. I. M. On the transfer of information from temporary to permanent memory. *Philosophical Transactions of the Royal Society*, Series B, 1983.

Craik, F. I. M., & Jacoby, L. L. Elaboration and distinctiveness in episodic memory. In L-G. Nilsson (Ed.), *Perspectives on Memory Research*. Hillsdale, N.J.: Erlbaum, 1979.

Craik, F. I. M., & Tulving, E. Depth of processing and the retention of words in episodic memory. *Journal of Experimental Psychology: General*, 1975, *104*, 268–294.

Crossman, E. R. F. W. A theory of the acquisition of speed-skill. *Ergonomics*, 1959, *2*, 153–166.

Daneman, M., & Carpenter, P. A. Individual differences in working memory and reading. *Journal of Verbal Learning and Verbal Behavior*, 1980, *19*, 450–466.

Daniel, T. C. Nature of the effect of verbal labels on recognition memory for form. *Journal of Experimental Psychology*, 1972, *96*, 152–157.

Danziger, K. The history of introspection reconsidered. *Journal of the History of the Behavioral Sciences*, 1980, *16*, 241–262.

Davis, R. Interactive transfer of expertise: Acquisition of new inference rules. *Artificial Intelligence*, 1979, *12*, 121–157.

Dawson, M. E., & Schell, A. M. Electrodermal responses to attended and nonattended significant stimuli during dichotic listening. *Journal of Experimental Psychology: Human Perception and Performance*, 1982, *8*, 315–324.

Dean, S. J., & Martin, R. B. Reported mediation as a function of degree of learning. *Psychonomic Science*, 1966, *4*, 231–232.

Deffenbacher, K. A. Eyewitness accuracy and confidence: Can we infer anything about their relationship? *Law and Human Behavior*, 1980, *4*, 243–260.

Dempster, F. N. Memory span: Source of individual and developmental differences. *Psychological Bulletin*, 1981, *89*, 63–100.

Deutsch, J. A., & Deutsch, D. Attention: Some theoretical considerations. *Psychological Review*, 1963, *70*, 80–90.

Dhanens, T. P., & Lundy, R. M. Hypnotic and waking suggestions and recall. *International Journal of Clinical and Experimental Hypnosis*, 1975, *23*, 68–79.

Dixon, N. F. *Preconscious Processing*. New York: Wiley, 1981.

Dixon, N. F. *Subliminal Perception: The Nature of a Controversy*. London: McGraw-Hill, 1971.

Dodd, D. H., & Bradshaw, J. M. Leading questions and memory: Pragmatic constraints. *Journal of Verbal Learning and Verbal Behavior*, 1980, *19*, 695–704.

Eccles, J. C. *The Understanding of the Brain* (2nd ed.). New York: McGraw-Hill, 1977.

Erdelyi, M. H. A new look at the new look: Perceptual defense and vigilance. *Psychological Review*, 1974, *81*, 1–25.

Erdelyi, M. A note on the level of recall, level of processing, and imagery hypotheses of hypermnesia. *Journal of Verbal Learning and Verbal Behavior*, 1982, *21*, 656–661.

Erdelyi, M. H., & Appelbaum, G. A. Cognitive masking: The disruptive effect of an emotional stimulus upon the perception of contiguous neutral items. *Bulletin of the Psychonomic Society*, 1973, *1*, 59–61.

Erdelyi, M. H., & Becker, J. Hypermnesia for pictures: Incremental memory for pictures but not words in multiple recall trials. *Cognitive Psychology*, 1974, *6*, 159–171.

Erdelyi, M. H., & Kleinbard, J. Has Ebbinghaus decayed with time?:

The growth of recall (hypermnesia) over days. *Journal of Experimental Psychology: Human Learning and Memory,* 1978, *4,* 275–289.

Ericsson, K. A., & Simon, H. A. Verbal reports as data. *Psychological Review,* 1980, *87,* 215–251.

Finke, R. A., & Kosslyn, S. M. Mental imagery acuity in the peripheral visual field. *Journal of Experimental Psychology: Human Perception and Performance,* 1980, *6,* 126–139.

Finke, R. A., & Schmidt, M. J. The quantitative measure of pattern representation in images using orientation-specific color aftereffects. *Perception & Psychophysics,* 1978, *23,* 515–520.

Fischhoff, B. Hindsight ≠ foresight: The effect of outcome knowledge on judgment under uncertainty. *Journal of Experimental Psychology: Human Perception and Performance,* 1975, *1,* 288–299.

Fischhoff, B. Perceived informativeness of facts. *Journal of Experimental Psychology: Human Perception and Performance,* 1977, *3,* 349–358.

Flavell, J. H. First discussant's comments: What is memory development the development of? *Human Development,* 1971, *14,* 272–278.

Flavell, J. H. Metacognitive development. In J. M. Scandura & C. Brainerd (Eds.), *Structural/Process Theories of Complex Human Behavior.* Alpen an den Rijn, Netherlands: Sitjoff & Noordhoff, 1978.

Flavell, J. H. Cognitive monitoring. In P. Dickson (Ed.), *Children's Oral Communication Skills.* New York: Academic Press, 1981.

Flavell, J. H., & Wellman, H. M. Metamemory. In R. V. Kail, Jr. & J. W. Hagen (Eds.), *Perspectives on the Development of Memory and Cognition.* Hillsdale, N.J.: Erlbaum, 1977.

Fowler, C. A., & Turvey, M. T. Skill acquisition: An event approach with special reference to searching for the optimum of a function of several variables. In G. A. Stelmach (Ed.), *Information Processing in Motor Control and Learning.* New York: Academic Press, 1978.

Fowler, C. A., Wolford, G., Slade, R., & Tassinary, L. Lexical access with and without awareness. *Journal of Experimental Psychology: General,* 1981, *110,* 341–362.

Gallistel, C. R. *The Organization of Action: A New Synthesis.* New York: Wiley, 1980.

Gardner, D. S. The perception and memory of witnesses. *Cornell Law Quarterly,* 1933, *18,* 391–409.

Glaser, M. O., & Glaser, W. R. Time course analysis of the Stroop phenomenon. *Journal of Experimental Psychology: Human Perception and Performance,* 1982, *8,* 875–894.

Glucksberg, S., & McCloskey, M. Decisions about ignorance: Knowing that you don't know. *Journal of Experimental Psychology: Human Learning and Memory*, 1981, *7*, 311–325.

Goldberg, E., Antin, S. P., Bilder, R. M., Jr., Gerstman, L. J., Hughes, J. E. O., & Mattis, S. Retrograde amnesia: Possible role of mesencephalic reticular activation in long-term memory. *Science*, 1981, *213*, 1392–1394.

Graf, P., Mandler, G., & Haden, P. E. Simulating amnesic symptoms in normal subjects. *Science*, 1982, *218*, 1243–1244.

Gray, C. R., & Gummerman, K. The enigmatic eidetic image: A critical examination of methods, data, and theories. *Psychological Bulletin*, 1975, *82*, 383–407.

Guenther, R. K., Klatzky, R. L., & Putnam, W. Commonalities and differences in semantic decisions about pictures and words. *Journal of Verbal Learning and Verbal Behavior*, 1980, *19*, 54–74.

Gummerman, K., Gray, C. R., & Wilson, J. M. An attempt to assess eidetic imagery objectively. *Psychonomic Science*, 1972, *28*, 115–118.

Haber, R. N. Twenty years of haunting eidetic images: Where's the ghost? *The Behavioral and Brain Sciences*, 1979, *2*, 583–594.

Haber, R. N. The impending demise of the icon: A critique of the concept of iconic storage in visual information processing. *The Behavioral and Brain Sciences*, 1983, *6*, 1–11.

Haber, R. N., & Haber, R. B. Eidetic imagery: I. Frequency. *Perceptual and Motor Skills*, 1964, *19*, 131–138.

Hart, J. T. Memory and the feeling-of-knowing experience. *Journal of Educational Psychology*, 1965, *56*, 208–216.

Hart, J. T. Memory and the memory-monitoring process. *Journal of Verbal Learning and Verbal Behavior*, 1967, *6*, 685–691.

Hasher, L., Attig, M. S., & Alba, J. W. I knew it all along: Or, did I? *Journal of Verbal Learning and Verbal Behavior*, 1981, *20*, 86–96.

Hasher, L., & Zacks, R. T. Automatic and effortful processes in memory. *Journal of Experimental Psychology: General*, 1979, *108*, 365–388.

Hermann, D. J. Know thy memory: The use of questionnaires to assess and study memory. *Psychological Bulletin*, 1982, *92*, 434–452.

Hintzman, D. L. Simpson's paradox and the analysis of memory retrieval. *Psychological Review*, 1980, *87*, 398–410.

Hirst, W., Spelke, E. S., Reaves, C. C., Caharack, G., & Neisser, U. Dividing attention without alternation or automaticity. *Journal of Experimental Psychology: General*, 1980, *109*, 98–117.

Holmes, G. The cerebellum of man. *Brain,* 1939, *62,* 11–30.

Jacoby, L. L., & Dallas, M. On the relationship between autobiographical memory and perceptual learning. *Journal of Experimental Psychology: General,* 1981, *110,* 306–340.

Jacoby, L. L., & Witherspoon, D. Remembering without awareness. *Canadian Journal of Psychology,* 1982, *36,* 300–324.

James, W. *The Principles of Psychology.* New York: Henry Holt, 1890.

Johnson, M. K. A multiple-entry, modular memory system. In G. H. Bower (Ed.), *The Psychology of Learning and Motivation: Advances in Research and Theory,* Vol. 17, New York: Academic Press, 1983.

Johnson, M. K., & Raye, C. L. Reality monitoring. *Psychological Review,* 1981, *88,* 67–85.

Johnson, M. K., Raye, C. L., Foley, H. J., & Foley, M. A. Cognitive operations and decision bias in reality monitoring. *American Journal of Psychology,* 1981, *94,* 37–64.

Kahneman, D., & Tversky, A. Subjective probability: A judgment of representativeness. *Cognitive Psychology,* 1972, *3,* 430–454.

Kahneman, D., & Tversky, A. On the psychology of prediction. *Psychological Review,* 1973, *80,* 237–251.

Keele, S. W. Movement control in skilled motor performance. *Psychological Bulletin,* 1968, *70,* 387–403.

Keele, S. Behavioral analysis of movement. In V. Brooks (Ed.), *Handbook of Physiology, Vol. 3: Motor Control.* Washington, D.C.: American Physiological Society, 1981.

Kinsbourne, M. Single-channel theory. In D. Holding (Ed.), *Human Skills.* New York: Wiley, 1981.

Klatzky, R. L. *Human Memory: Structures and Processes* (2nd ed). San Francisco: W. H. Freeman, 1980.

Klatzky, R. L. Visual memory: Definitions and functions. In R. Wyer, T. Srull, & J. Hartwick (Eds.), *Handbook of Social Cognition.* Hillsdale, N.J.: Erlbaum, in press.

Klatzky, R. L., & Erdelyi, M. The response criterion problem in tests of hyponosis and memory. Manuscript in preparation.

Kozlowski, L. T., & Bryant, K. J. Sense of direction, spatial orientation, and cognitive maps. *Journal of Experimental Psychology: Human Perception and Performance,* 1977, *3,* 590–598.

Kreutzer, M. A., Leonard, Sr. C., & Flavell, J. H. An interview study of children's knowledge about memory. *Monographs of the Society for Research in Child Development,* 1975, *40* (1, Serial No. 159).

LaBerge, D. Unitization and automaticity in perception. *Nebraska Symposium on Motivation 1980*. Lincoln: University of Nebraska Press, 1981.

Laurence, J–R, & Perry, C. Hypnotically created memory among highly hypnotizable subjects. *Science,* 1983, *222,* 523–524.

Leask, J., Haber, R. N., & Haber, R. B. Eidetic imagery in children: II. Longitudinal and experimental results. *Psychonomic Monograph Supplements,* 1968, *3* (3, Whole No. 35).

Leippe, M. R. Effects of integrative memorial and cognitive processes on the correspondence of eyewitness accuracy and confidence. *Law and Human Behavior,* 1980, *4,* 261–274.

Lieberman, D. A. Behaviorism and the mind: A (limited) call for a return to introspection. *American Psychologist,* 1979, *34,* 319–333.

Loftus, E. F. *Eyewitness Testimony*. Cambridge, Mass.: Harvard Univ. Press, 1979.

Loftus, E. F., & Loftus, G. R. On the permanence of stored information in the human brain. *American Psychologist,* 1980, *35,* 409–420.

Loftus, E. F., Miller, D. G., & Burns, H. J. Semantic integration of verbal information into a visual memory. *Journal of Experimental Psychology: Human Learning and Memory,* 1978, *4,* 19–31.

Long, G. M. Iconic memory: A review and critique of the study of short-term visual storage. *Psychological Bulletin,* 1980, *88,* 785–820.

MacKay, D. G. The problems of flexibility, fluency, and speed-accuracy trade-off in skilled behavior. *Psychological Review,* 1982, *89,* 483–506.

Malpass, R. S., & Kravitz, J. Recognition for faces of own and other race. *Journal of Personality and Social Psychology,* 1969, *13,* 330–334.

Mandler, G. *Mind and Emotion*. New York: John Wiley, 1975.

Mandler, G. Recognizing: The judgment of previous occurrence. *Psychological Review,* 1980, *87,* 252–271.

Marcel, A. J. Perception with and without awareness. Paper presented at the meeting of the Experimental Psychology Society, Stirling, Scotland, July 1974.

Marcel, A. Explaining selective effects of prior context on perception: The need to distinguish conscious and preconscious processes in word recognition. In R. Nickerson (Ed.), *Attention and Performance,* Vol. 8, Hillsdale, N.J.: Erlbaum, 1980.

Marcel, A. J. Conscious and unconscious perception: Experiments on visual masking and word recognition. *Cognitive Psychology,* 1983, *15,* 197–237. (a)

Marcel, A. J. Conscious and unconscious perception: An approach to the relations between phenomenal experience and perceptual processes. *Cognitive Psychology, 1983, 15,* 238–300. (b)

Marcel, A., & Patterson, K. Word recognition and production: Reciprocity in clinical and normal studies. In J. Requin (Ed.), *Attention and Performance,* Vol. 7. Hillsdale, N.J.: Erlbaum, 1978.

Marks, D. F. Visual imagery differences in the recall of pictures. *British Journal of Psychology,* 1973, *64,* 17–24.

McCauley, C., Parmelee, C., Sperber, R., & Carr, T. Early extraction of meaning from pictures and its relation to conscious identification. *Journal of Experimental Psychology: Human Perception and Performance,* 1980, *6,* 265–276.

McClelland, J. L., & Rumelhart, D. E. An interactive activation model of context effects in letter perception: Part 1. An account of basic findings. *Psychological Review,* 1981, *88,* 375–407.

McCloskey, M., & Egeth, H. E. Eyewitness identification: What can a psychologist tell a jury? *American Psychologist,* 1983, *38,* 550–563.

Merikle, P. M. Unconscious perception revisited. *Perception & Psychophysics,* 1982, *31,* 298–301.

Meyer, D. E., & Schvaneveldt, R. W. Facilitation in recognizing pairs of words: Evidence of a dependence between retrieval operations. *Journal of Experimental Psychology,* 1971, *90,* 227–234.

Meyer, D. E., & Schvaneveldt, R. W. Meaning, memory structure, and mental processes. *Science,* 1976, *192,* 27–33.

Miller, G. A. The magical number seven, plus or minus two: Some limits on our capacity for processing information. *Psychological Review,* 1956, *63,* 81–97.

Milner, B., Corkin, S., & Teuber, H.-L. Further analysis of the hippocampal amnesic syndrome. *Neuropsychologia,* 1968, *6,* 215–234.

Mischel, W., & Peake, P. K. Beyond deja vu in the search for cross-situational consistency. *Psychological Review,* 1982, *89,* 730–755.

Moray, N. *Attention: Selective Processes in Vision and Hearing.* New York: Academic Press, 1970.

Morris, C. D., Bransford, J. D., & Franks, J. J. Levels of processing versus transfer appropriate processing. *Journal of Verbal Learning and Verbal Behavior,* 1977, *16,* 519–533.

Moscovitch, M. Multiple dissociations of function in amnesia. In L. S. Cermak (Ed.), *Human Memory and Amnesia.* Hillsdale, N.J.: Erlbaum, 1982.

Murdock, B. B., Jr. *Human Memory: Theory and Data.* Hillsdale, N.J.: Erlbaum, 1974.

Muter, P. Very rapid forgetting. *Memory & Cognition,* 1980, *8,* 174–179.

Navon, D., & Gopher, D. On the economy of the human-processing system. *Psychological Review,* 1979, *86,* 214–255.

Neisser, U. *Cognitive Psychology.* New York: Appleton-Century, 1967.

Neisser, U. *Memory Observed.* San Francisco: W. H. Freeman, 1982.

Neisser, U., Novick, R., & Lazar, R. Searching for ten targets simultaneously. *Perceptual and Motor Skills,* 1963, *17,* 955–961.

Nelson, T. O., Leonesio, R. J., Shimamura, A. P., Landwehr, R. F., & Narens, L. Overlearning and the feeling of knowing. *Journal of Experimental Psychology: Learning, Memory and Cognition,* 1982, *8,* 279–288.

Newell, A. Reasoning, problem solving, and decision processes. The problem space as a fundamental category. In R. Nickerson (Ed.), *Attention and Performance,* Vol. 8. Hillsdale, N.J.: Erlbaum, 1980.

Newell, A., & Rosenbloom, P. S. Mechanisms of skill acquisition and the law of practice. In J. R. Anderson (Ed.), *Cognitive Skills and Their Acquisition.* Hillsdale, N.J.: Erlbaum, 1981.

Newell, A., & Simon, H. A. *Human Problem Solving.* Englewood Cliffs, N.J.: Prentice-Hall, 1972.

Newell, K. M. Some issues on action plans. In G. E. Stelmach (Ed.), *Information Processing in Motor Control and Learning.* New York: Academic Press, 1978.

Nisbett, R., & Ross, L. *Human Inference: Strategies and Shortcomings of Social Judgment.* Englewood Cliffs, N.J.: Prentice-Hall, 1980.

Nisbett, R. E., Wilson, T. D. Telling more than we can know: Verbal reports on mental processes. *Psychological Review,* 1977, *84,* 231–259.

Norman, D. A. *Memory and Attention,* New York: Wiley, 1969.

Norman, D. M. *Human Learning and Memory.* San Francisco: W. H. Freeman, 1982.

Norman, D. A., & Bobrow, D. G., On data-limited and resource-limited processes. *Cognitive Psychology,* 1975, *7,* 44–64.

Orne, M. T. On the social psychology of the psychological experiment: With particular reference to demand characteristics and their implications. *American Psychologist,* 1962, *17,* 776–783.

Orne, M. T., Soskis, D. A., & Dinges, D. F. Hypnotically induced testimony and the criminal justice system. In G. L. Wells & E. F. Loftus (Eds.), *Eyewitness Testimony: A Psychological Perspective.* Cambridge, England: Cambridge University Press, 1984.

Palmer, S. E. Visual perception and world knowledge; Notes on a model of sensory-cognitive interaction. In D. A. Norman, D. E. Rumelhart, & the LNR Research Group, *Explorations in Cognition.* San Francisco: W. H. Freeman, 1975.

Penfield, W. Consciousness, memory, and man's conditioned reflexes. In K. Pribram (Ed.), *On the Biology of Learning.* New York: Harcourt, Brace, & World, 1969.

Pew, R. W. Human perceptual-motor performance. In B. H. Kantowitz (Ed.), *Human Information Processing: Tutorials in Performance and Cognition.* Hillsdale, N.J.: Erlbaum, 1974.

Polanyi, M. *Personal Knowledge: Toward a Post-Critical Philosophy.* London: Routledge and Kegan Paul, 1958.

Posner, M. I. *Chronometric Explorations of Mind.* Hillsdale, N.J.: Erlbaum, 1978.

Posner, M. I., & Boies, S. J. Components of attention. *Psychological Review,* 1971, *78,* 391–408.

Posner, M. I., & Klein, R. M. On the functions of consciousness. In S. Kornblum (Ed.), *Attention and Performance,* Vol. 4. London: Academic Press, 1973.

Potter, M. C., & Faulconer, B. A. Time to understand pictures and words. *Nature,* 1975, *253,* 437–438.

Pratt, R. T. C. Psychogenic loss of memory. In C. W. M. Whitty & O. L. Zangwill (Eds.), *Amnesia* (2nd ed). London: Butterworths, 1977.

Purcell, D. G., Stewart, A. L., & Stanovich, K. E. Another look at semantic priming without awareness. *Perception & Psychophysics,* 1983, *34,* 65–71.

Putnam, B. Hypnosis and distortions in eyewitness memory. *International Journal of Clinical and Experimental Hypnosis,* 1979, *27,* 437–448.

Quillian, M. R. The teachable language comprehender: A simulation program and theory of language. *Communications of the Association for Computing Machinery,* 1969, *12,* 459–476.

Raibert, M. H. Motor control and learning by the state space model. Unpublished doctoral dissertation, Massachusetts Institute of Technology, Cambridge, Mass., 1977.

Read, J. D., & Bruce, D. Longitudinal tracking of difficult memory retrievals. *Cognitive Psychology,* 1982, *14,* 280–300.

Roediger, H. L., & Payne, D. G. Hypermnesia: The role of repeated testing. *Journal of Experimental Psychology: Learning, Memory, and Cognition,* 1982, *8,* 66–72.

Roediger, H. L., Payne, D. G., Gillespie, G. L., & Lean, D. S. Hypermnesia as determined by level of recall. *Journal of Verbal Learning and Verbal Behavior*, 1982, *21*, 635–655.

Rosch, E., Mervis, C. B., Gray, W., Johnson, D., & Boyes-Braem, P. Basic objects in natural categories. *Cognitive Psychology*, 1976, *8*, 382–439.

Rosenbaum, D. A., Kenny, S. B., & Derr, M. A. Hierarchical control of rapid movement sequences. *Journal of Experimental Psychology: Human Perception & Performance*, 1983, *9*, 86–102.

Ryan, C. Reassessing the automaticity-control distinction: Item recognition as a paradigm case. *Psychological Review*, 1983, *90*, 171–178.

Samuel, A. G. Phonemic restoration: Insights from a new methodology. *Journal of Experimental Psychology: General*, 1981, *110*, 474–494.

Samuels, S. J., LaBerge, D., & Bremer, C. D. Units of word recognition: Evidence for developmental changes. *Journal of Verbal Learning and Verbal Behavior*, 1978, *17*, 715–720.

Schachter, D. L. Feeling of knowing in episodic memory. *Journal of Experimental Psychology: Human Learning, Memory, and Cognition*, 1983, *9*, 39–54.

Schmidt, R. A. A schema theory of discrete motor skill learning. *Psychological Review*, 1975, *82*, 225–260.

Shaffer, L. H. Performances of Chopin, Bach, and Bartok: Studies in motor programming. *Cognitive Psychology*, 1981, *13*, 326–376.

Shallice, T. Dual functions of consciousness. *Psychological Review*, 1972, *79*, 383–393.

Shaughnessy, J. J. Memory monitoring accuracy and modification of rehearsal strategies. *Journal of Verbal Learning and Verbal Behavior*, 1981, *20*, 216–230.

Sheehan, P. W., & Tilden, J. Effects of suggestibility and hypnosis on accurate and distorted retrieval from memory. *Journal of Experimental Psychology: Learning, Memory, and Cognition*, 1983, *9*, 283–293.

Shevrin, H., & Dickman, S. The psychological unconscious: A necessary assumption for all psychological theory? *American Psychologist*, 1980, *35*, 421–434.

Shiffrin, R. M., Schneider, W. Controlled and automatic human information processing. II. Perceptual learning, automatic attending, and a general theory. *Psychological Review*, 1977, *84*, 127–190.

Smith, M. C., & Magee, L. E. Tracing the time course of picture-word processing. *Journal of Experimental Psychology: General,* 1980, *109,* 373–393.

Sokolov, E. N. Neuronal models and the orienting reflex. In M. A. Brazier (Ed.), *The Central Nervous System and Behavior.* New York: Josiah Macy Foundation, 1960.

Sperling, G. The information available in brief visual presentations. *Psychological Monographs,* 1960, *74,* (Whole No. 498).

Squire, L. R. Remote memory as affected by aging. *Neuropsychologia,* 1974, *12,* 429–435.

Squire, L. R., Cohen, N. J., & Nadel, L. The medial temporal region and memory consolidation: A new hypothesis. In H. Weingartner & E. Parker (Eds.), *Memory Consolidation.* Hillsdale, N.J.; Erlbaum, in press.

Stromeyer, C. F., III, & Psotka, J. The detailed texture of eidetic images. *Nature,* 1970, *225,* 346–349.

Stroop, J. R. Studies of interference in serial verbal reaction. *Journal of Experimental Psychology,* 1935, *18,* 643–662.

Swinney, D. A. Lexical access during sentence comprehension: (Re)consideration of context effects. *Journal of Verbal Learning and Verbal Behavior,* 1979, *18,* 645–660.

Terry, P., Samuels, S. J., & LaBerge, D. The effects of letter degradation and letter spacing on word recognition. *Journal of Verbal Learning and Verbal Behavior,* 1976, *15,* 577–585.

Thomson, D. M., & Tulving, E. Associative encoding and retrieval: Weak and strong cues. *Journal of Experimental Psychology,* 1970, *96,* 255–262.

Tulving, E. Subjective organization in free recall of "unrelated" words. *Psychological Review,* 1962, *69,* 344–354.

Tulving, E. Episodic and semantic memory. In E. Tulving & W. Donaldson (Eds.), *Organization and Memory.* New York: Academic Press, 1972.

Tulving, E., Schacter, D. L., & Stark, H. A. Priming effects in word-fragment completion are independent of recognition memory. *Journal of Experimental Psychology: Learning, Memory and Cognition,* 1982, *8,* 336–342.

Tulving, E., & Thomson, D. M. Encoding specificity and retrieval processes in episodic memory. *Psychological Review,* 1973, *80,* 352–373.

Turvey, M. T. On peripheral and central processes in vision: Inferences from an information-processing analysis of masking with patterned stimuli. *Psychological Review,* 1973, *80,* 1–52.

Turvey, M. T. Preliminaries to a theory of action with reference to vision. In R. Shaw & J. Bransford (Eds.), *Perceiving, Acting, and Knowing.* Hillsdale, N.J.: Erlbaum, 1977.

Turvey, M. T., Shaw, R., & Mace, W. Issues in the theory of action: Degrees of freedom, coordinative structures and coalitions. In J. Requin (Ed.), *Attention and Performance,* Vol. 7. Hillsdale, N.J.: Erlbaum, 1978.

Tversky, A., & Kahneman, D. Availability: A heuristic for judging frequency and probability. *Cognitive Psychology,* 1973, *5,* 207–232.

Tversky, A., & Kahneman, D. Belief in the law of small numbers. *Psychological Bulletin,* 1971, *76,* 105–110.

Tversky, A., & Kahneman, D. Judgment under uncertainty: Heuristics and biases. *Science,* 1974, *185,* 1124–1131.

Tversky, N. Distortions in memory for maps. *Cognitive Psychology,* 1981, *13,* 407–433.

Underwood, G. Memory systems and conscious processes. In G. Underwood & R. Stevens (Eds.), *Aspects of Consciousness,* Vol. 1. London: Academic Press, 1979.

Warren, R. M. Perceptual restoration of missing speech sounds. *Science,* 1970, *167,* 392–393.

Warrington, E. K., & Sanders, H. J. The fate of old memories. *Quarterly Journal of Experimental Psychology,* 1971, *23,* 432–442.

Weiss, P. Self-differentiation of the basic patterns of coordination. *Comparative Psychology Monographs,* 1941, *17* (No. 4).

Wells, G. L., Lindsay, R. C. L., & Ferguson, T. J. Accuracy, confidence, and juror perceptions in eyewitness identification. *Journal of Applied Psychology,* 1979, *64,* 440–448.

White, P. Limitations on verbal reports of internal events: A refutation of Nisbett and Wilson and of Bem. *Psychological Review,* 1980, *87,* 105–112.

Whitty, C. W. M., & Zangwill, O. L. Traumatic amnesia. In C. W. M. Whitty & O. L. Zangwill (Eds.), *Amnesia* (2nd ed). London: Butterworths, 1977.

Williams, M. D. The process of retrieval from very long-term memory. Technical Report No. 75, Center for Human Information Processing, University of California, San Diego, 1978.

Williams, M. D., & Santos-Williams, S. Method for exploring retrieval processes using verbal protocols. In R. Nickerson (Ed.), *Attention and Performance,* Vol. 8. Hillsdale, N.J.: Erlbaum, 1980.

Winograd, T. Frame representations and the declarative-procedural controversy. In D. Bobrow & A. Collins (Eds.), *Representation and Understanding*. New York: Academic Press, 1975.

Wood, F., Ebert, V., & Kinsbourne, M. The episodic-semantic memory distinction in memory and amnesia: Clinical and experimental observation. In L. Cermak (Ed.), *Human Memory and Amnesia*. Hillsdale, N.J.: Erlbaum, 1982.

Woodhead, M. M., & Baddeley, A. D. Individual differences and memory for faces, pictures, and words. *Memory and Cognition,* 1981, *9,* 368–370.

Woodworth, R. S. *Experimental Psychology*. New York: Holt, 1938.

Zelig, M., & Beidleman, W. B. The investigative use of hypnosis: A word of caution. *International Journal of Clinical and Experimental Hypnosis,* 1981, *29,* 401–412.

Index